Pan-Americanism
from Monroe
to the Present

Pan-Americanism
from Monroe
to the Present

A View from the Other Side
by Alonso Aguilar
translated by Asa Zatz
   New York and London

F,1418
·A 333
1968

First published in Mexico under the title of
*El Panamericanismo de la Doctrina Monroe
a la Doctrina Johnson*
© 1965 by Cuardernos Americanos

Revised English edition © 1968
by Monthly Review Press
116 West 14th Street, New York, N.Y. 10011
33/37 Moreland Street, London, E.C. 1, England

To Stella

The United States seems destined by Providence to plague America with misery in the name of liberty.

—Simón Bolívar

Among nations, as among individuals, peace is respect for the rights of others.

—Benito Juárez

Spanish America was able to save itself from the tyranny of Spain: and now . . . it must be said, because it is the truth, that the time has come for Spanish America to declare its second independence.

—José Martí

Introduction to the English Edition

The inter-American system has lived through many critical moments in the course of its turbulent history. The suspicious sinking of the "Maine" in Havana harbor in 1898 and the illegal seizure of the Panama Canal Zone in 1903 were dangerously threatening incidents. There were difficult times when United States Marines attacked the Mexican port city of Veracruz and occupied, *de facto*, country after country in Central America and the Caribbean. John Foster Dulles' "glorious victory" over the Guatemalan Revolution represented another grave moment for the system, as did the mercenary Bay of Pigs attack launched under the illusion of ousting the revolutionary government of Cuba. But perhaps the gravest crisis yet suffered by Pan-Americanism was that initiated by the unexpected United States aggression against the Dominican Republic in April, 1965.

The landing of thousands of United States soldiers in Santo Domingo and the raw and, in the end, clumsy attempt to transform unilateral aggression into a "collective intervention" and United States troops into an "inter-American military force"—under the pretext that the restoration of constitutional government in the Dominican Republic constituted a serious threat to the security of America—not only exposed the true nature of the Organization of American States (OAS) but very nearly brought about its demise. For a number of weeks, it seemed impossible that the OAS would ever manage to survive, and that it would be exceedingly difficult to repair the damage to the battered principle of self-determination of nations resulting from the aggression upon Santo Domingo.

In the last two years, however, Washington, as well as the

nations below the Rio Grande, have devoted themselves assiduously to the task of surmounting the crisis and of setting Pan-Americanism on its feet again and fortifying it. They have sought to accomplish this by laboriously trying to convince the peoples of Latin America that it is within the framework of the OAS, the Alliance for Progress [ALPRO], "representative democracy," economic integration, relentless struggle against international Communism, and the common market that our countries can develop most rapidly and raise their living standards. But while the most attractive watchwords of Pan-Americanism are repeated over and over again and the smooth and euphoric slogans which do credit to the professional skill of the ALPRO advertising men re-echo through the land, the stubborn facts remain. Poverty and underdevelopment persist, "gorillarchies" proliferate, violence and repression spread, and representative democracy shines by its absence. From Guatemala to Bolivia, the people are beginning to distrust the old and worn-out formulas that have not yet lifted them out of their backwardness and neglect and to seek other routes.

In order to cover, at least partially, the course run by Pan-Americanism since the Spanish edition of this book was published in 1965, a new chapter has been added to the English version. This covers such important events as the ominous House Resolution 560, the second Extraordinary Conference of the OAS, held in Rio de Janeiro at the end of 1965, the Tricontinental Conference of Havana in which representatives of the peoples of Latin America, Asia, and Africa met for the first time, and the special meeting in Panama early in 1966 at which it was proposed to renovate the OAS charter and provide the inter-American system with more effective instruments of action.

All that has taken place during this interval could not possibly be summed up in the scope of a few paragraphs. What can be said in brief, however, is that the Latin-American picture today is not what it was two years or even one year ago. Things have changed in more than one aspect. In the first place, United States strategy appears to be different from what it was in the time of President Kennedy. Following the aggression against Santo Domingo, there was a period in which the blindest kind of irrationality seemed to have irrevocably taken possession of United States officials. All they were interested in was bringing pressure to bear for the immediate establishment of the so-called Inter-American Peace Force. This was to be a permanent military body, not provided for in the Rio de Janeiro Treaty, which would have the thankless and sinister task of overriding the principle of nonintervention whenever and wherever the established order might be threatened. But when it was realized that such an attitude would serve no purpose other than to further undermine the OAS and reveal the imperialistic character of United States foreign policy, tactics began to change. New watchwords came in after the second Extraordinary Conference: forget the uncomfortable Santo Domingo episode; re-establish unity and mutual trust within the Organization; put aside the Inter-American Peace Force plan for the time being; and revise the OAS Charter to include the economic and social principles of the Alliance for Progress.

Accordingly, the third Extraordinary Conference and the eleventh Consultative Meeting of Foreign Ministers were held in Buenos Aires in February, 1967. The latter was also preparation for the Summit Meeting held the following April at Punta del Este. Despite the fact that certain inevitable discrepancies among the American governments came to the fore in the last two meetings mentioned, it was nevertheless agreed to amend the Bogotá Charter and to make economic integration and the establishment of a Latin-American common market the hub of joint and hemispheric effort.

This emphasis upon the integration scheme, which came as a surprise to some observers, seemed to indicate that the United States was adopting a new policy and that, in the future, instead of insisting on military and security questions, it would finally cooperate in the grand task of promoting Latin-American economic development. However, the actual facts provide no grounds for such optimism. On the one hand, the United States conception of integration is a far cry from what it should be in order to contribute effectively to the genuine industrialization of Latin America. The integration Washington talks about, which receives the unconditional backing even of Wall Street, is hardly the means that would help Latin America to resist the incursions of the great foreign monopolies. Quite the contrary. This integration is a mechanism for enabling precisely those foreign monopolies to expand at will in the Latin-American subcontinent in search of economies of scale within the framework of a free trade policy, of tax grants, and of generous financial backing from international organizations. On the other hand, while it was agreed until recently, even in official circles, that there could be no integration without economic planning, now nobody, or hardly anybody, is interested even in the moderate institutional reforms mentioned so much in the program of the Alliance for Progress launched a few years ago by John F. Kennedy—an alliance which, it is apparent, has become an alliance for the preservation of the status quo.

To think that regional integration alone will open new horizons for the economies of our countries is to fail to understand the basic problems that must be faced today. Actually, regional integration is fundamentally a policy by which Latin America's governments, instead of granting facilities to their national enterprises, allow the great foreign monopolies to "export" a small portion of their productive installations and processes to Latin-American countries.

Achievement of the most modest economic integration on a national scale, to say nothing of the international, presupposes a considerable measure of planning. At the same time, the most modest attempts at planning require the overcoming of Latin-American structural obstacles which block the rapid increase of the productive potential or its even moderately rational utilization. Actually, none of this is feasible unless a break is made with the stifling dependence upon imperialism whose principal expression today in the legal, economic, political, and even cultural spheres is Pan-Americanism. Nor does that imperialism relax the pressures it brings to bear inside and outside the system through the police and other means of repression. As *The New York Times* accurately reported recently, "In the countries of practically all United States allies, CIA agents have made themselves known to the friendly government and work in close collaboration with its members, local espionage, and the police."*

It will not be difficult for the reader to catch the change in tone of inter-American relations. Outwardly, stress is placed on the need for integration. Yet instead of raising aloft the banner of "peaceful revolution" which was unfurled not long ago in answer to the Cuban model of "violent revolution," universities are now being taken over by force, the international espionage network is being extended, and the protests of the youth and the most genuine expressions of popular dissatisfaction are smothered as though they were the gravest crimes deserving the most severe punishment.

The truth of the matter is that the inter-American system is facing a decisive test. The people feel that their problems are becoming more acute than ever and that the announcement of reforms that are never forthcoming or the making of never-fulfilled promises leads nowhere. Enough talk! Enough windy speeches about democracy in places where the most elementary human rights are disregarded! To speak of democracy and freedom when only repression and violence exist is a searing irony and in as bad taste as talking of rope in the house of the hanged.

The façade of peace in Latin America is cracking. Armed struggle is being discussed in many countries and foci of rebellion are beginning to crop up. Guerrillas operate in Guatemala, Venezuela, Colombia, Bolivia. Not long ago, the magazine *Visión* wrote: "There is evidently nothing more artificial than these guerrillas." What a profound lack of understanding

---

* *El Día*, Mexico, February 24, 1967.

of the state of affairs in Latin America is revealed in these
words!

Of course, popular discontent, growing disagreement, the
spreading conviction that the violence of the oligarchies in
power must be answered by violence on the part of the people,
the deep disillusionment with pseudo-democratic forms, and
finally, the turn to guerrilla warfare where the routes of civic
action have been completely blocked are not at all artificial.
Rather, what is artificial, shallow, and even grotesque is to
consider that the struggle for a profound social transformation, which arises as a genuine historical imperative and begins
to consolidate in various forms, is a foreign conspiracy which
can be halted and, in the long run, liquidated through "intelligent" police action and increased use of other repressive
measures. These are, indeed, violent and contrary to human
rights and revive inquisitorial practices and fascist methods
such as the burning of books deemed subversive by the new
Torquemadas.

The Latin-American peoples are beginning to learn the
lessons of history. They are beginning to grasp the reasons for
their backwardness and to recognize the unquestionable possibilities of overcoming it. And even though they lack proper
political organization and, alienated, often follow interests
that are not their own, their activity is becoming more and
more determined and forceful. It is true, of course, that new
victims are constantly being felled, and many men and women
are being deprived of their freedom and even their lives. But
the fight goes on despite repression, intimidation, and even
armed force. With all the stumbling, hesitation, and inevitable
errors, the cause of freedom and full independence for Latin
America is making headway as an irreversible fact which
neither the Marines nor police forces of the dictatorships can
stop.

Nobody thinks that the road will be easy or that victory
is around the corner. We Latin Americans have lived in
the vortex of a long and bloody struggle which has taught us

that social progress is won through effort and sacrifice and even the dramatic tribute of blood. As Major Ernesto Guevara recently phrased it: "We cannot harbor the illusion—we have no right to harbor it—that freedom can be won without fighting."

ALONSO AGUILAR

June, 1967

Contents

Contents

Foreword

On April 28, 1965, the President of the United States, Lyndon B. Johnson, ordered the landing of 400 Marines in Santo Domingo in order to forestall the imminent triumph of the people in overthrowing a weak and unpopular military dictatorship. It is possible that many Latin Americans, although naturally concerned about this development, were momentarily unable to gauge its significance and grave implications. But only a few days sufficed—one week, actually—for the aggressive policy of the United States to be exposed and for Latin America to realize that imperialism was still imperialism despite the rhetoric of the foreign ministers of the OAS and despite the good intentions, wishful thinking, and repeated pronouncements endorsing the principles of self-determination and nonintervention.

When the 400 Marines sent to "protect the lives and property of U.S. citizens residing in the Dominican Republic" grew into an aggressive force of almost 40,000 fully armed troops, Mr. Johnson's hypocrisy no longer deceived anyone. His motivations, in fact, were basically the same as those which had prompted Mr. Blaine (Secretary of State during President Harrison's Administration) to propose the first Pan-American Conference; which caused Theodore Roosevelt to invent a "revolution" in Panama in order to seize control of the Isthmus; which led President Taft to use the American flag to protect United States monopolies seeking raw materials and markets outside their own country; and the very same which Calvin Coolidge defended in repeated declarations to the effect that the rights of United States investors, and the obligation of the government in Washington to protect them,

19

stood above the principles of self-determination and respect
for national sovereignty.

The aggression against the Dominican Republic together
with the so-called Johnson Doctrine, which purports to be its
rationale, have highlighted the profound crisis which the inter-
American system is undergoing, revealing in a single stroke
that the policy of anti-Communism inherited from Churchill
and Truman, instead of serving the national interests of Latin
America or safeguarding the security of the continent, constitutes a grave threat to the sovereignty of these nations and
is no more than a crude device for maintaining the status quo.

Anti-Communism, favorite weapon of the Pentagon strategists, the U.S. State Department, representatives to the
Organization of American States, and the Latin-American
oligarchies and "gorillarchies"—its most recent form is the
Johnson Doctrine—is not an instrument against armed aggression by a foreign power. It is, rather, the principal weapon
being used by imperialism and its allies to hold back social
or political progress in Latin America and other parts of the
world where the people seem ready to transform present socio-
economic conditions.

For almost a century and a half, the United States has used
the Monroe Doctrine to prevent European countries from
exporting their political systems to the Americas. By extension, under the Johnson Doctrine, the nations of Latin America are prevented from choosing their form of government and
so do not even control their own destinies. As events have
dramatically shown in the Dominican Republic and before
that in Brazil, Cuba, and Guatemala, Latin Americans are in
a sorry plight. If a Latin-American nation, in the full exercise
of its sovereignty, chooses a government or type of social organization unfavorable to United States interests or unacceptable to privileged local minorities, the result is either violent
unilateral intervention by the United States or the emergence
of a politician or army officer disposed to betray his people by

crying out for Pan-Americanism to enter into immediate action in defense of the indefensible.

After the criminal aggression against the Dominican Republic and the creation of the repressive "inter-American military force," it occurred to me that it might be useful to make a rapid study of the historical development of Pan-Americanism, recapitulating and bringing up to date its main episodes for the benefit of the young people entering the struggle for the emancipation of Latin America. Accordingly, with the assurance of Jesús Silva Herzog that I could count on the hospitality of his publishing house, Cuadernos Americanos, I set out to write these pages.

I feel obliged to warn the reader, however, that this is not a study in depth but rather a rapid survey of the complex and turbulent processes which I believe to be the principal causes of the economic backwardness and dependent position of Latin America.

Scholars in the fields of Pan-Americanism and of the history of relations between Latin America and the United States will probably not find much of interest and may even disagree with a good part of what is said here. But this essay is not addressed to the specialist. Rather, I had ordinary people in mind; the youth, who often seem to forget that the peoples of Latin America have not yet achieved full independence; teachers in primary and higher schools who, though they do contribute to the creation of a Latin-American consciousness, sometimes become skeptical and disillusioned; and the workers and peasants of the vanguard who are beginning to understand better than those looking down on them from ivory towers that their miserable conditions will change only when the revolutionary struggle is organized and carried to a successful conclusion.

If this book helps in any way to clarify the true character of Pan-Americanism, if it contributes to the understanding of the manner in which the imperialism behind it has succeeded

in holding back our development, and, finally, if it serves in
the smallest degree to stimulate the struggle for the full
emancipation of Latin America, I shall feel amply rewarded.

ALONSO AGUILAR

Mexico, August, 1965

1. Bolívar and Monroe

In 1823, the majority of the countries of Latin America were already independent. Nevertheless, although republican arms had triumphed decisively on the fields of battle, the new nations still had to consolidate their independence, obtain formal recognition, and achieve cohesiveness. The victories of the Latin-American peoples opened new horizons for democratic ideas and social and political change in America, but these developments were regarded with hostility and distrust by the Holy Alliance, the combination of European oligarchies determined to preserve the old social order which the French Revolution had begun to raze to the ground.

England quickly understood what the birth of independent Latin-American republics meant for Europe. Aware that the old and anachronistic system of colonial relations would crumble, it saw an excellent opportunity to profit by establishing commercial relations with the newly independent countries. Consequently, between 1815 and 1823 England countered the colonialist designs of the Holy Alliance by asserting the principle of nonintervention in Latin America. The Prime Minister, George Canning, emphasized the importance of trade with the new countries in his statement, "England will be a workshop and Latin America its farm."[1]* In order to insure this business for the British fleet—but at the same time fearful lest the United States and France launch a policy of territorial expansion in Latin America—Mr. Canning proposed an agreement with these two governments that would guarantee the peace and tranquility of the continent.

In mid-1823, the astute Mr. Canning initiated negotiations

* For notes, see end of each chapter.

23

to strengthen the British Empire in its efforts to expand its
overseas markets; these finally took the form of several concrete proposals submitted to the United States, based on the
following premises:

> We consider it impossible for Spain to recover the colonies;
> We consider recognition of those colonies as states to be a
> matter of time and circumstances;
> We will not impede any arrangement between the colonies
> and the motherland reached by friendly means;
> We, on our part, have no designs on any portion of the said
> colonies.[2]

The United States government studied the British proposal.
President Monroe consulted former Presidents Jefferson and
Madison and heard the counsel of his closest advisers. Jefferson, who was already thinking in 1820 of "an American system
independent and disconnected from Europe,"[3] accepted the
British proposal in principle despite his reservations about
England and his own openly annexationist designs on Cuba.
Madison, convinced that it should be United States policy to
"break up the crusade which the European powers are seeking
to carry out in America,"[4] also accepted and suggested *de facto*
intervention by the United States even if this meant crossing
the theoretical meridian which, according to Jefferson, should
separate the new continent from the old.

President Monroe took a dubious view of Canning's proposal, fearing that acceptance would place the United States
in a subordinate role. But the person frankly opposed was John
Quincy Adams, Monroe's Secretary of State, who shrewdly
recognized that what England sought was a commitment from
the United States that it would expressly refrain from a policy
of territorial annexation. Confident, in the first place, that the
Holy Alliance would not attempt to restore the Spanish empire, and conscious of United States interest in Texas, Adams
maintained that "the United States should not relinquish its
future freedom of action" or sign permanent pacts, but should
maintain a flexible policy adaptable to any contingency.

In November of the same year, the Russian Ambassador to Washington handed the government a note which, in essence, contained a reiteration and justification of the policy of the Holy Alliance. Monroe immediately drafted a reply vigorously censuring Europe's interventionist policy. But when this was presented to Congress a few days later, the view that prevailed was Adams' once again, and so definitively that the presidential message might just as well have become known as the "Adams Doctrine" instead of the Monroe Doctrine.

In his message, President Monroe declared that the nations of America were not open for colonization by any European power, and that any intervention aimed at dominating or controlling them would be considered "the manifestation of an unfriendly disposition toward the United States."[5]

The Monroe Doctrine postulated that: "It is impossible that the allied powers should extend their political system to any portion of either continent without endangering our peace and happiness. . . . It is equally impossible, therefore, that we should behold such interposition, in any form, with indifference."[6]

Superficially, this doctrine might appear to be an instrument intended to encourage the independent development of Latin America in the face of the designs of the old European monarchies; its true implications were quite different. The United States was not really interested in strengthening the independence of Latin America, and much less in getting involved in a war with Spain. The real motive behind Monroe's policy was that of laying down the foundations of United States hegemony on the continent, an objective that was not originally his. In addition to the fact that the idea that Europe should not intervene in American affairs was basically a British policy, the idea of extending United States influence was shared by others, beginning with John Quincy Adams. Even Jefferson had intimated as much as early as 1786 when he said: "Our Confederation must be considered the nucleus from which the settlers of the north and south of the Americas will come forth."[7] And Hamilton had asserted: "We may expect before long to become the arbiters of Europe and America, being able to tilt the scale . . . in accordance with the dictates of our interests."[8]

Barcia Trelles [an eminent Spanish jurist, especially distinguished in the field of international law] was therefore correct in saying: "The United States in 1823 did not save the independence of [Latin] America; it played the part of the leader of a firing squad who delivers the *coup de grace* to what is already practically a corpse. . . . European claims on the new world were no longer viable. . . ."[9]

It has often been said that apart from contributing to the consolidation of Latin-American independence, the Monroe Doctrine also incorporated the best of Bolivarian ideology and contributed to the laying of the foundations of Pan-Americanism in the 1826 Congress of Panama where, for the first time, representatives of the new American republics met together. This notion is often even carried to such lengths that the Congress of Panama is considered the birthplace of Pan-Americanism, and the Pan-American Union and the Organization of American States as the embodiments of the ideals of the Liberator. Nevertheless, few things could be less true. The United States was never in favor of the underlying principles or goals of the Latin-American alliance which Bolívar fought so hard to realize, and which was also fostered by his illustrious precursor, Francisco de Miranda, and supported by O'Higgins, San Martín, and Monteagudo.

Beginning in 1814, Bolívar began to let his deep interest in uniting the new republics be felt. In a letter written that year, he emphasized the importance of "a union of all southern America in a corps of nations."[10] The following year he insisted: "It is a noble idea to attempt to form one single nation out of the whole new world with a single bond joining the parts to each other and to the whole. Inasmuch as they have the same origin, language, customs, and religion, they must . . . have one government which would join together the various states to be formed." However, realizing the geographic and political objections to the ideal of a single Latin-American nation, Bolívar leaned toward a confederation, declaring: "How wonderful it would be if the Isthmus of Panama could be for us what Corinth was for the Greeks."[11]

In 1818, the Liberator returned to the same theme: "There should be one homeland for all Americans, since we have always been perfectly unified." And, immediately afterward, he indicated that as soon as Venezuelan independence was won, ". . . we shall pursue with the liveliest interest on our part the realization of the American Pact which, by casting all our republics into one body politic, will present an America to the world of a majesty and grandeur unparalleled among the nations of old."[12]

In his letter of December, 1824, to the governments of Colombia, Rio de la Plata, Chile, Mexico, and Guatemala, Bolívar set out to implement his old ideal:

> After fifteen years of sacrifice consecrated to the freedom of America, it is time that the interests and relations linking the American republics, previously Spanish colonies, to one another had a solid foundation to prolong, eternally if possible, the duration of their governments. . . . To establish such a system, to consolidate power into one great body politic, is the exercise of a supreme authority. . . . An authority capable of commanding such respect can exist only in a meeting of plenipotentiaries appointed by each of our republics and meeting under the aegis of the victory won by our arms over the Spanish power.[13]

The meeting was finally held in Panama in 1826, but obviously it did not represent what Bolívar and other Latin-American leaders had envisioned. In the first place, some countries did not attend and others failed to grasp the importance of the meeting; secondly, the United States, England, and the Netherlands were also invited; and finally, circumstances prevailing at the time evidently conspired against the success of a meeting of any great scope with the attendant obligations implied.

The responsibility for inviting the United States is attributed to Francisco de Paula Santander: "The Liberator did not invite the United States because his idea was to form a Confederation of Latin-American Nations. It was General Santander who, as Vice-President of Colombia, invited the United States, England, and the Netherlands without consulting anyone. This amounted to vitiating the essence of the Liberator's concept."[14]

The important point is that, since United States foreign policy had other objectives, it was impossible, within the framework of the Congress of Panama, to achieve the union of sister nations as originally envisioned.

Bolívar strove for the unity and mutual defense of the new republics, goals to which were added, a short time later, the liberation of Cuba and Puerto Rico. The United States, on the other hand, was interested solely in keeping Europe—particularly England—out of America, and in contributing to the frustration of Cuban and Puerto Rican independence, as Henry Clay definitively established in his instructions to the United States delegates to the Congress of Panama.

Professor Lloyd Mecham is quite right in saying that Henry Clay was the main propagandist of "an American system of which the United States would be the center and in which all of Latin America would act with it." And he is justified in adding that while "the Liberator would have restricted his amphictyonic union to the newly created Spanish-American states and would have had them contract formal alliances for their mutual protection, President Adams, while favoring an American system which embraced all the Americans, balked at permanent entanglements with the new states and wanted no part in their war against Spain"—much less in the liberation of Cuba and Puerto Rico.[15]

Bolívar and Santander always thought that the Congress of Panama should reach clear-cut resolutions on the course to be pursued to insure the independence of both countries. Adams, on the other hand, stated unequivocally when he accepted the invitation to the Congress that he was doing so "only to the extent compatible with the neutrality which we have no intention of breaking."[16]

Some authors claim that the inclusion of the United States at Panama was actually due to Bolívar's sense of "continentalism," overlooking the fact that his concept was one of "Spanish-American continentalism." The Mexican diplomat, Cuevas Cancino, for example, asserts that "it may be said that the Liberator's concept is clearly so broad that it encompasses the entire continent. . . . Contractually, Pan-Americanism originates in the Spanish-American countries; from them, it extends to include the Portuguese, then the free Anglo-Saxons, and finally, according to Bolívar's concept, the whole continent."[17]

I don't agree. I consider that there is irrefutable evidence to the contrary which proves that what always interested Bolívar was the close union of the nations fighting for freedom from Spain, and which makes it equally clear that other nations were included in the Congress of Panama for incidental tactical reasons completely removed from the Bolivarian ideal. And although the Liberator personally felt that England's presence at the Congress of 1826 would be of greater use to the new republics in their struggle against Spain and the Holy Alliance than to England herself, who would unquestionably obtain commercial advantages, it is evident that her inclusion had nothing to do with the idea of turning Panama into what Corinth had been for the Greeks.

Furthermore, the Liberator took it upon himself to make it absolutely clear that the Congress of Panama had not lived up to his expectations. In a letter to José Antonio Páez (Venezuelan general, 1790–1873), he said: "The Congress of Panama, which might have been an admirable institution had it been more efficacious, is the same as that mad Greek who sought to steer passing ships from a rock. Its power will be a shadow and its decrees merely suggestions."[18] And in a letter to Santander, he wrote: "I see the Congress of the Isthmus as a theatrical performance."[19]

Although it was not always easily discernible, two opposing concepts of the security, freedom, and peace of the continent frequently came into conflict: the Pan-Americanism of Jefferson, Monroe, and Clay, forerunner of the system of Latin-American subordination established toward the end of the century; and the Latin-Americanism of Bolívar, San Martín, and Morelos which stood for the struggle of their people for full independence.

Notes

[1] *Industria Argentina y Desarrollo Nacional* by Arturo Frondizi, Buenos Aires, 1957, p. 27.

[2] *Doctrina de Monroe y cooperación internacional,* by Camilo Barcia Trelles, Madrid, 1931, p. 82.

[3] *Ibid.,* p. 56.

[4] *Ibid.,* p. 94.

[5] *Encyclopedia of the Social Sciences,* Vol. 10, p. 630.

[6] *El Panamericanismo, doctrina y práctica imperialista* by Ricardo A. Martínez, Buenos Aires, 1957, p. 72.

[7] *Nacionalismo y socialismo en América Latina* by Oscar Waiss, Buenos Aires, 1961, p. 41.

[8] *Ibid.,* p. 69.

[9] Camilo Barcia Trelles, *op. cit.,* p. 127.

[10] *El Panamericanismo. Una moderna interpretación,* by Luis Hernández Solís, Mexico, 1944, pp. 28, 29.

[11] *Intervención,* by Isidro Fabela, Mexico, 1959, p. 178.

[12] *Ibid.,* p. 179.

[13] R. A. Martínez, *op. cit.,* pp. 40–41.

[14] *El Superhombre,* by J. A. Cova, Caracas, 1949, p. 35, quoted by Hernández Solís, *op. cit.*

[15] *The United States and Inter-American Security, 1889–1960,* by Lloyd Mecham, Texas, 1961, pp. 46–67.

[16] Isidro Fabela, *op. cit.,* p. 186.

[17] *Bolívar: El ideal Panamericano del Libertador,* by Francisco Cuevas Cancino, Mexico, 1951, p. 164.

[18] Hernández Solís, *op. cit.,* p. 43.

[19] *Obras Completas de Simón Bolívar,* Letter of July 8, 1826, Vol. II, p. 428.

2. United States Territorial and Economic Expansion

After the Congress of Panama, attempts to create a Latin-American system or a continental organization were abandoned, although an effort was made at the Conference of Tacubaya in 1833 to continue the work initiated by the Congress of Panama. Also an Ibero-American Customs League was planned, but was not accepted by the United States. Several decades elapsed before the idea of the creation of a collective regional body, whose character would be the expression of America's historical development from the 1830's to the 1880's, was again discussed.

Latin America developed slowly and irregularly during that period, stagnating at times, and even retrogressing. After political independence was won, the social struggle sharpened everywhere. To some degree, this was the inevitable consequence of the anachronistic colonial order inherited by the new states, which would not be liquidated for many years since there were powerful sectors interested in preserving it. Despite this, however, new forces gradually gained ground and these succeeded in entrenching themselves in power toward the middle of the century in the wake of a liberal movement which renovated ideas and institutions from Mexico to Chile and Argentina. But the long years of instability, internecine struggles, economic crisis, and postponing action frequently led to the complete abandonment rather than the rapid development of the liberal movement, thereby making it impossible for Latin America to organize and promote economic growth. Furthermore the free trade or, in fact, "Open Door" policy adopted at this time put England, in particular, in a position to make the most of her advantage. The growing flow of trade consolidated British power, promoted the industrialization of the British Empire, and extended its influence in America; but at the same time it gave rise to a competition ruinous to the Latin-American countries, which had barely reached a stage of incipient development within a framework of totally unfavorable international economic relations.

While these were the conditions south of the Rio Grande, quite a different situation developed in the United States. There a process of expansion unprecedented in the New World took place.

With the end of the Revolutionary War and the signing of the Peace Treaty of 1783 recognizing its independence, the United States initiated a westward march which multiplied its territory many times within a few short years. This expansion took place in six stages, primarily in the half-century between 1803 and 1853:[1]

1. In 1803, Louisiana was purchased from France, which lost Haiti at the same time; the expansionist designs of France in America thereby suffered a severe blow. The United States paid the ridiculous sum of $15 million for a vast territory of almost one million square miles.

2. The second step was taken in 1819. After repeated border incidents and long drawn out negotiations, Spain ceded her possessions east of the Mississippi and renounced her rights to Oregon. As a result, the United States acquired the territory of Florida (38,700 square miles) for $5 million.

3. In 1846, it was Oregon's turn. The joint occupation by England and the United States ended under pressure from the latter and an agreement was reached whereby the United States added another 286,500 square miles to its already enormous territory, an area which today comprises the states of Oregon, Washington, Idaho, and parts of Wyoming and Montana.

4. In the same year war began against Mexico, a frankly unjust war which completely exposed the aggressiveness of United States policy and the violent character of its territorial expansion.

The Mexican War aroused mixed reactions in the United States. While President Polk considered it "a proper occasion to reiterate and reaffirm the principle avowed by Mr. Monroe, and to state my cordial concurrence in its wisdom and sound policy,"[2] many other voices were raised against the war. The labor unions openly criticized the annexation of Texas, and important sectors of industry also condemned the government's policy.

The severest criticisms were heard in the Congress. Senator Corwin of Ohio declared: "If I were a Mexican I would tell you: 'Have you not room in your own country? . . . If you come into mine, we will greet you with bloody hands and welcome you to hospitable graves.' " Another congressman from Ohio called it "a war against an unoffending people without adequate or just cause, for the purpose of conquest. . . . I will lend it no aid, no support whatever. I will not bathe my hands in the blood of the people of Mexico, nor will I participate in the guilt of those murders which have been and will hereafter be committed by our army there."[3] Lincoln also protested against the war. He considered it unnecessary and unconstitutional and wrote that the blood of the war, like the blood of Abel, cries out against it. And Ulysses S. Grant wrote many years later: "I do not think there was ever a more wicked war than that waged by the United States in Mexico."[4]

5. As a result of the aggression against Mexico, the United States first acquired Texas and shortly after, in 1848, another large slice of territory. Altogether, the United States incorporated some 945,000 square miles—a vast area which today includes the states of Texas, Arizona, New Mexico, California, Nevada, Utah, and part of Wyoming. After appropriating

these lands, to which it had no right whatsoever, the United States paid $26.8 million for them—as though this made the annexation legal.

6. Finally in 1853, through the Gadsden Purchase, the United States acquired another small strip of border land of some 45,000 square miles in the Mesilla Valley for the absurd sum of $10 million.

To sum up, in the course of half a century, the United States increased its territory tenfold—not including Alaska. That is to say, nearly 2.3 million square miles were acquired by various means for the "reasonable" price of a little over $50 million.

This policy of territorial expansion was determined by the growing commercial, industrial, and agricultural power and interests of the United States. The Revolutionary War played a very important role in accelerating capitalist development. Then, spurred by truly exceptional circumstances (the right historical moment, a democratic climate, the absence of a deep-rooted feudal structure, an effective industrial development policy, vast natural resources, a growing, hard-working population with a relatively high educational level, and rapid technological progress), the United States economy was transformed within a few decades.

Starting in the third and fourth decades of the seventeenth century, the fight against the Indians for control of the land was carried on with unprecedented ruthlessness. By the beginning of the nineteenth century, the white man had succeeded in driving his victims across the Mississippi. Many Indians had to die so that their lands could pass into the hands of the new entrepreneurs.

As industrial capitalism continued to transform the United States and increase its ability to exploit new territories and new peoples, not only the Indians but also the French, British, and Spanish felt the force of this new power. Its full fury, however, was to be felt by Latin America.

Notes

[1] Cf. *U.S. Foreign Policy: Shield of the Republic* by Walter Lippmann, Boston, 1943, pp. 13–16.
[2] *Dollar Diplomacy*, by Scott Nearing and Joseph Freeman, New York, 1925, p. 239. (Reprinted by Monthly Review Press, New York, 1966.)
[3] *We, The People* by Leo Huberman, New York, 1964, pp. 132–133.
[4] Quoted in *The Nation*, October 16, 1967, p. 357.

3. *Imperialism and Pan-Americanism*

The world economic structure underwent basic changes during the second half of the nineteenth century. England, whose economic development had begun almost a century before that of other European countries, consolidated and extended its power, wealth, possessions, and overseas spheres of influence. Germany's initiation as an industrial nation began in the decade following the Franco-Prussian War. France made considerable progress despite the military defeat suffered in 1870, and rapidly ceased being an agricultural country. Even Russia and Japan, which had been trailing behind, began to awaken after long centuries of lethargy and neglect. However, it was the transformation of the economy of the United States that had the greatest impact upon Latin America.

In the course of a few decades, United States capitalism went through a phase which must be understood in order to grasp what the United States economy signifies today and the manner in which inter-American relations have developed over the last eighty years. That phase is marked by the following developments: (1) The anarchic growth of production within a competitive system greatly stimulated the concentration of capital; (2) this concentration in turn brought about the formation of large companies, particularly in industry and later in banking and other services; (3) the growth of these large companies modified and at the same time sharpened competition, culminating in the appearance of the great monopolies or trusts which succeeded in dominating the most varied fields of the economy; (4) national monopolies, after integrating themselves vertically and horizontally in all the industrial countries, began to cross their own frontiers and seek contacts abroad, thus giving rise to the big international cartels and to the increasing exports of merchandise and, especially, of capital; (5) more or less simultaneously, industrial enterprises combined or merged with the banks, producing the new financial oligarchy; and, (6) the drive to expand, obtain markets, secure cheap materials, win strategic positions, and do more and better business everywhere implied, on the one hand, the sharpening of crises and of the internal social struggle and, on the other, the occupation of large territories, especially in Asia and Africa, frequent international conflicts, and the heightening of rivalry among the major powers. This sums up the essentials of the imperialist stage which began toward the end of the last century, and in which the Pan-American system made its appearance precisely at that point when the United States, after completing its own internal expansion, emerged as a great power and set out to dominate the continent and extend its influence even as far as the most remote Asiatic countries.

In 1881, James Blaine, Secretary of State in the Garfield Administration, proposed a Pan-American conference because he considered that "things had ripened and the moment was nearing when the United States could displace Europe in trade with America."[1]

It was evident from the start that, in terms of trade, the United States had come of age. The days when Monroe had opposed European colonization of America were past. It was now possible to take a further step and practically eliminate Europe from the industrial, commercial, and financial business of the continent. And, although the Monroe Doctrine had never really been in force at any time, from this point forward it was to be brandished as a foreign policy weapon of the United States.

The idea of a continental conference did not arouse great

enthusiasm in Latin America. The most that could be said was that although the plan of creating a purely defensive confederation had been forgotten, Alberdi's idea [Juan Bautista Alberdi, 1810–1884, Argentine lawyer and political thinker], which had been proposed some years earlier in Santiago, Chile, still remained alive:

> The American states do not think, nor have they ever thought, that the meeting of an assembly . . . could be capable, solely by its own efforts, of extricating them from the situation they are in; they believe, however, that among the many possible ways of eradicating the general ills, one of the most effective might be a meeting of America at a given moment in one place in order to become fully cognizant of their condition, . . . of their ills, and of means by which they might find a way of bringing about a change for the better through their joint efforts.[2]

What sort of reunion did Alberdi have in mind? A Pan-American Congress such as Blaine was to propose years later? No. Like Bolívar, half a century before, Alberdi meant a Latin-American meeting. He had said: "Despite the frequency with which I have made use of the word *continental*, I am one of those who feels that the general congress should be attended only by the American republics of Spanish origin." Reinforcing his thesis, he had added: "Since the end of the War of Independence against Spain, we do not know what America thinks of itself or its destiny; absorbed in routine work and problems, it seems to have lost sight of the common objectives to be achieved once the old bonds of oppression were broken."[3]

The conference proposed by Blaine did not take place in 1881, or for almost a decade. But when the vast domestic market inside the United States began to be insufficient and the rate of profit began to decline, when the powerful industrial trusts, the mining and railroad interests, and the banks demanded new spheres of influence, and when the government entered the struggle for power against the old European regimes, the Pan-American system emerged. "Pan-Americanism was born in Washington in 1889, was promoted from Washington, and was received by Latin America, in the beginning, with coldness not unmixed with distrust. Annexation was not its purpose; it pursued a different objective, that of insuring the industrial domination of the United States in the new world."[4]

The invitation to the first Pan-American Conference issued by the United States government stated that the conference was called to consider measures that "shall tend to preserve the peace and promote the prosperity of the several American states," and "for the purpose of discussing and recommending for adoption to their respective Governments some plan of arbitration for the settlement of disagreements and disputes that may hereafter arise between them, and for considering questions relating to the improvement of business intercourse and means of direct communication between said countries, and to encourage such reciprocal commercial relations as will be beneficial to all and secure more extensive markets for the products of each of said countries."[5]

In line with this purpose, James Blaine, the new Secretary of State, proposed the creation of a customs union in order to attain "trade reciprocity approaching a large-scale free trade system," at a moment when the Latin-American countries were beginning to adopt protectionist measures but when the United States, on the other hand, secure in its increasing economic power, was beginning to do without protective measures and to unfurl the banner of free trade.

The Latin Americans, for their part, proposed that the conference adopt, as a basic principle of American international law, a resolution establishing the following:

1. Aliens shall enjoy all the civil rights enjoyed by nationals. . . .
2. The nation neither requires nor recognizes any obligations or responsibilities of aliens beyond those established by the Constitution and laws for the native born in the same conditions.

The reasons which impelled Latin America to bring up such questions are understandable. The flow of foreign capital into the continent was growing rapidly; foreign investors frequently sought to obtain privileges of all kinds and in cases of conflict appealed to their home governments for support, in violation of the principles of national sovereignty. But the Latin-American proposal was not approved by the United States, which prompted Fabela to comment: "There have been two opposing trends since the first Pan-American Conference: that of preserving . . . the absolute sovereignty of independent states [as against] the interference of the great Nordic power in their internal affairs and . . . that of non-approval of an unobjectionable principle of law, namely, that of the equality of states and the respect which aliens and nationals should enjoy equally in whatever country they happen to be."[6]

Nevertheless, the conference agreed to accept an arbitration mechanism for settling possible conflicts or differences which was never put into practice—and it was also agreed to create an International Union of American Republics which would be represented by a bureau with headquarters in Washington; this was later to become the Pan-American Union.

The positions put forward by the United States in 1889–1890 were subsequently strengthened. The country's huge domestic economic development, its enormous wealth and drive, the conviction of its statesmen and businessmen that it was constantly getting stronger and that its destiny was to expand its domains, all contributed to creating a self-sufficient and aggressive international policy. In 1896, when England illegally seized a portion of Venezuelan territory adjoining British Guiana, President Cleveland, perhaps to put Europe on notice, declared: "At the present moment, the United States, in fact, enjoys sovereign rights over the continent and its will has the force of law." Two years later, in a state of full

expansionist euphoria, Senator Beveridge attributed the path
United States policy was taking to destiny, saying:

"The trade of the world must and shall be ours. . . . We
will cover the ocean with our merchant marine. We will build
a navy to the measure of our greatness. . . . Our institutions
will follow our flag on the wings of our commerce. And American law, American order, American civilization, and the
American flag, will plant themselves on shores hitherto bloody
and benighted, but by those agencies of God henceforth to be
made beautiful and bright."[7]

The war against Spain in 1898 enabled the United States,
in Senator Beveridge's sublime phrase, to make "beautiful and
bright" new territories. The outcome of that war and of the
treaty, signed in Paris, which ended it, could hardly have been
more advantageous to the United States. The Philippines,
Guam, and Puerto Rico passed into its possession, thus enabling it to realize its old ambitions of transforming the Caribbean into a United States lake and of having a strategic base in
the East. The victory over Spain was decisive in bolstering the
thesis of "manifest destiny." In fact, on the signing of the
treaty, Senator Platt said: "Every expansion of our territory
has been in accordance with the irresistible law of growth. . . .
The history of territorial expansion is the history of our nation's progress and glory. It is a matter to be proud of."[8] And
one of the United States signers of the treaty wrote in 1899:
"We are today the most wealthy nation on the face of the
globe. . . . The statesmanship of the present and the future
is to extend our commercial relations and secure markets for
our marvelous surplus productions."[9]

By virtue of this, how could anyone possibly speak of United
States imperialism? The uncontainable expansion of the
United States had nothing whatsoever to do with her foreign
policy, nor with the transition of a competitive commercial
and industrial economy into a finance capitalism in which
monopolies rapidly took over. It was merely the workings of

"natural laws," of the "inexorable law of growth," of a "divine mandate" to make "beautiful and bright" other lands with the United States flag, civilization, institutions, and dollars.

Notes

[1] R. A. Martínez, *op. cit.*, p. 86.

[2] "Conveniencia y objetos de un Congreso General Americano," by Juan Bautista Alberdi, in *Hispanoamérica en lucha por su independencia*, edited by Jesús Silva Herzog, Mexico, 1962, p. 83.

[3] J. B. Alberdi, *op. cit.*, pp. 97–98, 100.

[4] *La política exterior norteamericana de la postguerra*, by C. Barcia Trelles, Valladolid, 1924, p. 20.

[5] *The International Conferences of American States, 1889–1928*, by James Brown Scott, New York, 1931, pp. 3 ff.

[6] Isidro Fabela, *op. cit.*, pp. 195–196.

[7] *Beveridge and the Progressive Era*, by Claude G. Bowers, New York, 1932, p. 69.

[8] Nearing and Freeman, *op. cit.*, p. 256.

[9] *Ibid.*, p. 257.

4. From "Big Stick" to "Philosophy of Liberty"

The policy of "manifest destiny" probably reached its zenith during the administration of William McKinley, who tried to conceal the hegemonic objectives of the United States in its relations with Latin America behind a front of generous "big-sister" concern. The United States was merely carrying out its destiny—a destiny which, apparently, expressed itself in a mandate to intervene in other countries when the interests of civilization so demanded. As for McKinley's gratuitous "guardianship," initiated under his "big-sister" policy, it can only be said that it never materialized but soon became, instead, the "Big Stick" policy made notorious in America by the picturesque and headstrong Theodore Roosevelt.

The determination of the United States to control the Gulf of Mexico and the Caribbean began to take shape as far back as the early days of independence. Toward 1820, Jefferson already considered that Cuba "could be the most interesting possible addition to our system of states."[1] At the time of the Congress of Panama, it was evident that the United States was not disposed to back the independence of Cuba and Puerto Rico precisely because she hoped to control them herself as soon as the time was ripe. In 1850, when the Clayton-Bulwer Treaty was signed, the United States and England agreed to build a neutral non-militarized canal in Nicaragua which would facilitate trade between the Atlantic and the Pacific. In 1880, however, the United States government forgot about the treaty and decided that the canal would be totally North American. And a few years later the Caribbean became the principal target of United States expansion. As Admiral

Mahan said, "One thing is sure—the Caribbean is the strategic key to two great oceans, the Atlantic and the Pacific, our main maritime frontiers."[2]

United States penetration of the Caribbean took two avenues: commercial and military. At the outset, particularly after 1880, United States companies began establishing themselves in Cuba, Puerto Rico, Jamaica, and Central America to produce bananas, tobacco, and various minerals; and toward the end of the century the United Fruit Company, for one, was already a large owner of their main agricultural exports. On the other hand, hardly had Cuba launched its struggle for independence than the United States intervened to prevent a popular victory which undoubtedly would have led to the emancipation of the island and to blocking United States expansionist policy.

The incidents the United States took advantage of to justify its military intervention in Cuba are well known. On February 15, 1898, the United States cruiser "Maine," at anchor in the port of Havana, suddenly and mysteriously exploded. Spain was blamed and a few weeks later the United States government sent an ultimatum, the prologue to war. Hypocritically, the United States recognized the Cuban people's right to independence, but at the same time introduced the so-called Teller Amendment, which decreed "United States military occupation in order to pacify the island of Cuba."[3]

Shortly afterwards, the Teller Amendment was converted into the Platt Amendment and, in 1903, it became a treaty for the lease of naval and military bases by which the United States was able to add new strategic possessions in the Caribbean. It was so obvious that the real aim of the Platt Amendment was to deprive the Cuban people of the independence they had won in the struggle initiated by José Martí and Gómez that General Leonard Wood, commander of the United States forces there, declared:

> Of course, the Platt Amendment has left Cuba with little or no independence . . . and the only course now is to seek annexation. . . . It cannot enter into certain treaties without our con-

sent, nor seek loans beyond certain limits, and it must maintain the sanitary conditions established for it, all of which makes it very evident that it is entirely in our hands and I do not believe that a single European government would consider it other than what it is, a virtual dependency of the United States.[4]

Concurring with General Wood, Congressman Corliss of Michigan indicated, when the amendment was introduced in the House, that he was voting for the amendment . . . "because I believe that the adoption thereof will insure the continuance of our sovereignty" over Cuba.[5] And Leland W. Jenks points out that the Cubans agreed: "A cartoon of the time, published in the leading Cuban daily, *La Discusión*, portrayed Cuba nailed to the cross between General Wood and McKinley as the thieves, while Platt, as Roman centurion, presented the Amendment sponge upon a spear."[6]

After the Platt Amendment came the Reciprocal Trade Treaty of 1903, which was to contribute greatly to Cuba's underdevelopment since it guaranteed the United States preferential tariffs in its trade with Cuba. All of this made it quite clear, as Martí once said, that "neither charity nor the velvet glove are natural United States products."[7]

After 1898, Cuba and Puerto Rico, whose freedom Latin-American patriots had fought for during the preceding three-quarters of a century, continued to be dominated by the United States under the Monroe, Clay, and John Quincy Adams doctrines. Spain lost both territories, but they were merely shifted from colonial to semicolonial status, now dependent upon an even more brutal imperialism. With good reason, Bolívar wrote to Santander in 1825, "I do not believe the Americans should participate in the Congress of the Isthmus." And a few days later, "I am also very glad that the United States is not entering the federation."[8]

The purpose of extending United States domination and assuring effective control of the Caribbean did not terminate with the seizure of Cuba and Puerto Rico. On a global scale, the conquest of the Philippine Islands was very significant. The policy of carrying the United States flag and trade to the

Orient began with expansion to the West (Oregon and Washington)—where it was hoped to establish important outposts for overseas commerce—and with Commodore Perry's expedition to Japan in 1853 which provided the United States with its first military bases in the Far East. In 1859, Midway Island was acquired; in 1867, Alaska was purchased from Russia; and a few years later the Hawaiian Islands were annexed. The strategic value of the Philippines was indisputable as much from a commercial as from a military standpoint—they represented to the United States what Hong Kong did to England. Senator Beveridge stated: "Just beyond the Philippines are China's illimitable markets. . . . The power that rules the Pacific is the power that rules the world. And, with the Philippines, that power is and will forever be the American Republic."[9]

With regard to China, the United States backed the so-called Open Door policy which, in essence, consisted of opening China's doors to the great Western imperialist powers on an equal footing, while closing all doors to any real development and in that way subordinating China to the interests of the big trusts and the governments of England, the United States, Germany, and Japan.

United States expansion into the Pacific, which took it first to Manila Bay and then to the very center of eastern Asia, suddenly augmented the strategic value of the ocean and especially of a canal which would link the Pacific to the Atlantic. The idea of a Central American canal was not new—it had been put forward as early as 1850. Now it took on special importance because the United States merchant fleet had grown and imperialist rivalry was beginning to sharpen. Another factor was the emergence of what Mahan called United States "Asiatic domination" at a time when the country's main ports and industrial zones were on the Atlantic, thus necessitating a route which would assure easy access to the Pacific. Furthermore, a canal was becoming necessary to establish communication by water between the two coasts of the

United States: although land traffic was constantly growing in volume, it was costly and often difficult.

So the process of transforming the Caribbean into an "American Mediterranean" continued. After the death of McKinley, it fell to his belligerent successor, Theodore Roosevelt, to tackle the job in Panama. The history of the canal and United States ambitions concerning it probably started in 1846 with the signing of the Mallarino-Bidlack Treaty which granted franchises for transporting goods and persons across the Isthmus. In the same year, a contract known as the Stephens-Paredes Agreement was signed which authorized a group of United States investors to build a trans-isthmian railroad. In 1850 came the Clayton-Bulwer Treaty, by which England sought to prevent her exclusion by the United States from the benefits of a Central American canal. In 1900 and 1901, the situation was modified by the Hay-Pauncefote Treaties which England did not sign in the end because she felt that the conditions granted the United States were too favorable. Furthermore, since the end of the century, France had also been interested in building a canal. Fearing that some of these efforts might be successful, the United States Congress passed in 1902 the Spooner Act empowering the President to immediately negotiate the construction of an interoceanic canal. As a result, conversations were initiated with Colombia—since the Isthmus of Panama was part of that country—and in the following year, the Hay-Herrán Treaty set down conditions for the construction and operation of the canal. However, these conditions were so unacceptable that the Colombia Congress rejected them completely, considering them a grave threat to its sovereignty.

Faced with Colombia's flat refusal, the United States decided to try other tactics to obtain the canal. Exploiting an old separatist sentiment among certain sectors of the population of the Isthmus, and taking advantage of the dissatisfaction left in the wake of the "Thousand Days War" between liberals and conservatives, the United States formulated a plan for an independent Panama as a United States protectorate under the Hay-Herrán Treaty.

"The plan was carried out," wrote David M. Turner, "but the United States . . . charged a high price for her aid by imposing upon the infant Republic of Panama a treaty even more unfair than the Hay-Herrán Treaty, even though the latter was the basis for the new agreement, the Hay-Bunau-Varilla Treaty."[10]

The Panamanian government, despite its weakness and its obvious subordination to the United States, nevertheless decided to make some counterproposals. When the State Department learned of this, it rushed through the signing of the preliminary text and "amidst this net of intrigues," as the Panamanian jurist Ricardo Alfaro said, "the negotiation and closing of the Canal Treaty was consummated in three days."[11] Referring to the fact that the Treaty of 1903 granted the United States a strip of Panamanian territory in perpetuity, over which it could exercise absolute control, he correctly observed:

It is quite evident what the sovereignty of Panama has been reduced to if jurisdiction and the other powers deriving from sovereignty are exercised by the United States to the complete exclusion of the Republic of Panama. The answer to this question is the key: the sovereignty of Panama is limited to all those aspects in which the rights, power, and authority deriving from it are not necessary for the specific objective of the construction, maintenance, sanitation, and protection of the canal.[12]

Once more, the United States imperialistic interests prevailed over the interests of a small sovereign state. The Panamanian "insurrection" was essentially the product of the decision to get the Panama Canal immediately and never before had such quick action been taken. The Panamanian "revolution" was announced in Washington practically before it broke out, and the United States—a nation traditionally reluctant to grant recognition to another nation born out of a revolutionary movement—gave its blessing to a "*de facto* republican government constituted without opposition from the people."[13]

The dénouement of the Panama episode made quite clear the meaning of President Roosevelt's words a few days earlier: "Privately, I freely say to you that I should be delighted if Panama were an independent state, or if it made itself so at this moment."[14] And at the height of the crisis, when the United States government's attitude had given rise to understandable perplexity, Roosevelt said arrogantly, "I took the Canal Zone and let the Congress debate; and while the debate goes on the Canal does also."

But Roosevelt's "formal" statement justifying the Panama adventure was different. It was a rationale based on the theory of "manifest destiny" and on the vague and abstract mandate given the United States by "civilization" to "coerce a nation which, by its 'selfish' actions, stood in the way of measures that would benefit the world as a whole."[15]

As United States expansion gained impetus, the Pan-American system, born in Washington shortly before, also began to grow in importance. In 1901, at the second Pan-American Conference held in Mexico, the need was discussed for submitting the conflicts which might arise among nations of the continent to arbitration (compulsory, according to some of the Latin-American countries, and voluntary, according to the United States). Once again, an understandable discrepancy arose in connection with the rules about aliens and international claims, inasmuch as Latin America was defending its threatened sovereignty and the United States was backing the interests and demands of its investors abroad.

The convention on aliens approved at the Mexico conference confirmed the draft prepared at the 1889 meeting (see pp. 39–40). A precept was also added to the general principles whereby, in case of claims, foreigners must bring suit before the competent national courts and not resort to the diploma-

tic protection of their governments except in cases of "manifest denial of justice, abnormal delays, or evident violation of
the principles of international law."

Regarding this convention, Isidro Fabela [Foreign Minister
of Mexico under President Carranza, 1918–1920, and a member of the International Court of Justice] pointed out that
"the United States delegates were not opposed . . . nor did
they approve it," and as for the arbitration treaty proposed at
the conference, he remarked that "the United States, stubbornly opposed to international arbitration from the start, did
not sign this treaty."[16]

When the third Pan-American Conference met in Rio de
Janeiro in 1906, Latin-American resentment against the
United States and its non-agreement were evident.

> The "taking" of the Panama Canal . . . the exercise with "the
> big stick" of a self-appointed international police power in the
> Caribbean, and the assuming of customs control in the Domin-
> ican Republic—all these evidences of the new Yankee impe-
> rialism created a profound distrust of the United States; this is
> readily understandable, particularly if it is recalled that President
> Roosevelt in his Annual Message to Congress on December 6,
> 1904, had broadened the scope of the Monroe Doctrine with an
> addition according to which the United States would intervene,
> by force, if it became evident that their [the Latin-American
> countries] inability or unwillingness to do justice at home and
> abroad had violated the rights of the United States or had in-
> vited foreign aggression to the detriment of the entire body of
> American nations.[17]

That is, just as President Polk had amended the Monroe
Doctrine half a century earlier in order to "legitimize" annexa-
tions like that of Texas, Theodore Roosevelt attempted to
justify aggressions under his own Administration and those
which were to follow in country after country by adding what
became known as the Roosevelt Corollary. According to this
new amendment proclaimed by Roosevelt in 1904, lack of
order in any country called for the intervention of civilized

states, "and in the Western Hemisphere the adherence of the United States to the Monroe Doctrine may force the United States, however reluctantly . . . to the exercise of an international police power."[18]

Under this new formula, the "divine mandate" which had spurred the United States to grow unceasingly and to intervene in the affairs of other countries in accordance with the philosophy of "manifest destiny," was transformed into a supposedly legal doctrine which was unilaterally formulated by a United States President before the Congress of his country; and the Roosevelt Corollary (as will be shown below) was to play a major role in United States relations with Latin America.

The main political problems of the continent were not taken up at the Rio conference of 1906; much less was there discussion of topics whose airing would have exposed the true nature of United States policy. Just as nothing was said at the Mexico meeting about the military intervention in Cuba or the Platt Amendment, no mention was made in Rio of the plunder of Panama or of the crude expedient resorted to by Theodore Roosevelt to try to justify his aggressive policy. The principal concern of the United States continued to be to defend its investors and, in the same way that it had rejected the Calvo Doctrine before, in Rio it refused to accept the Drago Doctrine.*

After the armed aggression against Venezuela in 1902, allegedly justified by Venezuela's failure to pay her debts, Drago wrote:

---

* The Calvo doctrine, named for Carlos Calvo, a distinguished Argentine internationalist, provided that foreigners be subject to the legislation and courts of the nation in which they reside. Although it was strongly upheld by various Latin-American delegations at the first Pan-American Conference in 1889, the Calvo Doctrine was not accepted by the United States.

The Drago Doctrine was named for Luis María Drago, who was Argentine Minister of Foreign Relations in 1902 when he first expounded his doctrine that intervention or coercion by a creditor nation against a debtor nation, in order to force fulfillment of a financial commitment, was a violation of national sovereignty.

The capitalist who provides money to a foreign state always takes into account the resources of the country in question, and the greater or lesser probability that the obligations will be met without problems. . . .

Also, the creditor knows that he is making a contract with an entity, and it is an inherent condition of all sovereignty that no executory process may be brought against it, since such a way of collection would compromise its very existence, invalidating the independence and action of the respective government. Impetuous and immediate collection of a debt by the use of force at a given moment can only bring ruin to weak nations and the absorption of their governments by the powerful of the earth.[19]

However, in place of this legally and politically unobjectionable Latin-American thesis, in 1907 the Court at the Hague— to which the Rio conference had passed on the problem— accepted the so-called Porter Doctrine, which made it *conditionally* illegal to use force as long as the debtor country agreed to arbitration and to accept the resulting decision.

Nothing was essentially changed by the fourth Pan-American Conference held in Buenos Aires in 1910. It was agreed to create the Pan-American Union and the United States delegates once more contrived to prevent delicate political problems from being discussed; in fact, although armed interventions had taken place between 1906 and 1909, nothing was said about them. One thing that could not be avoided, however, was growing discouragement with Pan-Americanism. In 1913, the Argentine Ambassador to Washington declared, "There is no Pan-Americanism in South America; it exists only in Washington." And a Buenos Aires newspaper said: "We reject Pan-Americanism, which is but a hollow mockery for us South Americans."[20]

What explains this attitude? What had happened to inter-American relations after Panama? What was the essence of the foreign policy of the Taft and Wilson Administrations and how did it differ from that of Roosevelt and McKinley?

In the first place, the so-called Roosevelt Corollary was not the expression of United States policy by only one particular

Administration. Roosevelt's policy of "speak softly but carry a big stick" was followed by what became known as "dollar diplomacy," based on the supposed right of the United States to intervene in the affairs of other countries and the decision to open the way for United States investors abroad. Shortly after he became president, Taft said about the Caribbean: "It is essential that the countries within that sphere shall be removed from the jeopardy involved by heavy foreign debt, and chaotic national finances, and from the ever-present danger of international complications due to disorder at home. Hence, the United States has been glad to encourage and support American bankers who were willing to lend a hand to the financial rehabilitation of such countries."[21]

In line with this policy, which differed only in form from that of the Big Stick, interventions and abuses perpetrated by the United States multiplied between 1906 and 1916 under the widest range of pretexts. One author lists the following:

1906–09. Second intervention in Cuba, led by General Charles E. Magoon.

1907. Fiscal intervention in the Dominican Republic, establishing a tax collector's office there.

1907. Imposition upon the Central American republics of the so-called peace and friendship treaties, all signed in Washington.

1909. Breaking off of relations with Nicaragua and the first armed intervention there.

1912. Third military intervention in Cuba to "protect American lives and interests" on the pretext of racial and political differences.

1912. Marines and infantry sent to the Dominican Republic to reinforce the intervention and "prevent revolutions."

1912–1925 (actually, until 1933). More warships, marines, and infantry sent to Nicaragua to reinforce the armed intervention.

1913. Intervention by the United States Ambassador, Henry Lane Wilson, in the internal affairs of Mexico. He was directly responsible for the success of the *Ciudadela* military coup during the *Decena Trágica* (the so-called Ten Tragic Days of bloodshed in February, 1913, during the presidency of Madero), and, it has been suggested, for the murder of President Madero and Vice-President Pino Suárez.

1914. Imposition of the Bryan-Chamorro Treaty by which the United States obtained the inter-oceanic route in Nicaragua in perpetuity.

1915. Armed attack on, invasion, and occupation of Haiti.

1916. Ratification by the United States Senate of the Bryan-Chamorro Treaty with Nicaragua, despite the decision handed down by the Central American Court.

1916. Invasion of Mexico by General Pershing's "punitive expedition."[22]

It would be impossible within the limited scope of this study to cite all the vicissitudes of each of the above-mentioned aggressions. What does seem clear enough, however, is that it was not fate, as Senator Morgan claimed in 1906, that drove the United States into its unbridled expansionist race. Rather, it was imperialism and the intent to extend its domains farther and farther, outside the continent as well as within, sometimes for purposes of political strategy and sometimes for overtly commercial and financial ends. Actually, the Roosevelt Corollary became United States foreign policy in 1905 when a foreign receivership which lasted for four years was arbitrarily foisted on the Dominican Republic. However, the procedure chosen in each case varied according to the circumstances, ranging from the "financial protectorate," whereby several United States bankers took charge of the operation of the "protected" country, to armed aggression involving high-ranking military officers and Marines.

It is also important to emphasize that United States policy on the continent did not change appreciably from either the first Roosevelt to Taft or from Taft to Wilson.

Woodrow Wilson came to the presidency of the United States in mid-1912 as a reformer and a generous and idealistic man disposed to put an end to injustice and ruthlessness in international relations and to make the principle of peaceful negotiation of differences prevail. Wilson repudiated "dollar diplomacy" and in one of his first declarations on Latin-American affairs in March, 1913, he said: "One of the main objectives of my Administration will be to cultivate and earn the confidence of our sister republics in Central and South America, and by all appropriate and honorable means to promote the common interests of the peoples of the two continents."

In October of the same year, he made the following statement regarding the Latin-American countries before an assembly of businessmen: "When it comes to equality and honor we must prove that we are their friends and champions. You cannot be friends under any conditions other than equality. You cannot be friends at all except under honorable conditions."[23]

Such declarations led people to think that, in fact, United States policy would change and that the "philosophy of freedom" or the doctrine of the New Freedom, as it used to be called, would usher in a new era in inter-American relations. When the Treaty of Bogotá was signed in 1914 to indemnify Colombia for damages suffered during the events leading up to the opening of the Panama Canal, the United States government took a moderate and respectful tone toward Colombia. In his message to Congress in 1915, President Wilson spoke of "a moral society in continental affairs" in which there would be no "pretense of tutelage or ideas of guardianship, but rather . . . a full and honorable partnership."[24]

However, the cautious, calm, and almost always restrained language of President Wilson and his Secretary of State, William Jennings Bryan, did not correspond with the crude and violent reality of United States imperialism, examples of which followed one upon another without interruption, in apparent obedience to a pathological drive to impose "United States democracy" upon the continent by force.

The fifth Pan-American Conference, initially planned for 1914, was finally held in Chile in 1923. In 1915, however, at the first Pan-American Financial Conference in Washington, Bryan insisted that the United States did not desire a single yard of land in any country; all it wanted was hemispheric solidarity.[25]

What it really wanted, however, was not the solidarity but

the subordination of the hemisphere. In proof of this, we have seen how between 1906 and 1916 the United States went about the task of establishing military bases in Central America and the Caribbean as its investors, first under the wing of "dollar diplomacy" and then as crusaders of President Wilson's New Freedom, increased their business, getting troops to help whenever necessary to "clean up" the economies of the countries in which they were investing. Cuba was practically an occupied country between 1906 and 1909; Santo Domingo was the victim of armed intervention in the name of the Santo Domingo Improvement Company; and the same fate befell Nicaragua as a consequence of the voracity of Brown Brothers & Co. and Seligman & Co.

The invasion of Veracruz took place in 1914. Not long before the landing of troops, Congressman Oscar Underwood, House leader, said: "For more than a year, we have been facing a state of turmoil, a state of disorder . . . of anarchy in the Republic of Mexico that has threatened the lives and properties of the citizens of the United States. . . . [We must] compel a decent respect. . . . [for] the flag that makes it safe for an American to put his foot on foreign soil."[26]

In summary, economic penetration followed on the heels of diplomatic and political interference and even military aggression. As the historian Spykman said: "By virtue of the Monroe Doctrine, Marines were landed, elections supervised, customs controlled, central banks administered, and *de facto* protectorates established over various Caribbean states. . . . The only ones to whom the so-called painless United States imperialism has seemed painless have been ourselves. The Central American republics undoubtedly found modern bookkeeping lessons backed up by bayonets quite painful."[27]

Or, as Victor Perlo put it, "The American people have been raised on the comfortable myth that United States armies are non-aggressive; that American business enterprise penetrates the world by means of peaceful competition and service to consumers."[28]

Reality has been quite different. As the power of the United States and the great trusts grew, domination of Latin America was stepped up and violations of national sovereignties multiplied.

Referring to Wilson, Link wrote: "There is a certain irony in this whole story. The man who . . . abhorred the very thought of using force in international relations became the first president in the history of the United States to use violence in imposing its will on nations which were, at least theoretically, free and sovereign."[29]

And the banner unfurled by Wilson in support of his policy was always the Monroe Doctrine with the Roosevelt Corollary tacked on. Part and parcel of this was growing United States opposition to European investments on the continent and the idea, expressed by Bryan in 1915 and Wilson himself on several occasions, of the "Pan-Americanization" of the old Doctrine and of getting all the nations of America to accept it.

The attempt to "Pan-Americanize" the Monroe Doctrine was unsuccessful. Although some of the countries, more through weakness than conviction, appeared ready to accept Wilson's thesis, the truth won out in the end, the same truth that had been coming through for a long time and showing up the real nature of the Doctrine. Wilson's failure also demonstrated that though Monroeism continued to flourish in the United States, the Bolivarian ideal was still alive in Latin America. The ideas so brilliantly put forward by the illustrious Argentine President, Roque Sáenz Peña, as delegate to the first Pan-American Conference in 1889, had retained their force from the Rio Grande to the Río de la Plata. Referring to the Monroe Doctrine, he said at the time:

> In its legal aspect, this declaration does not amount to a doctrine; it is an action, but not a system or an international or political theory. . . .
> Since the New World is made up of free and independent republics, not one of them, so far, has achieved sufficient international stature to represent the rest, or to determine their

destinies with relation to the Old World. That imaginary line which seeks to perpetuate itself on the waters dividing two continents, is not a doctrine but a parody of the famous encyclical which divided the world in two parts, conferring flimsy and precarious sovereignties over them. . . .

The statements on the political system of the peoples of America could not be graver: . . . they entail curtailment of their autonomous powers to choose the forms of government best suited to their natures, interests, and sociological conditions without being pressed into the particular mold of one nation which exercised the same right when it was constituted, as the others now demand and exercise. . . . In the name of what principle could such intervention for the purpose of dictating the political organization of the new states be justified? Were they even consulted? Did there happen to have been a continental plebiscite which consecrated the institutional system of the Republic of the North to be extended and spread throughout a hemisphere?

And, after pointing out that prohibitions placed on forms of governments ostensibly have no warrant to justify them other than "the happiness enjoyed in the United States under its system," Sáenz Peña remarked sharply that "national happiness is not a Yankee monopoly nor the exclusive invention of the Constitutional Convention of Philadelphia."[30]

Sáenz Peña's concept of Monroeism was not an isolated or individual notion. Rather, he echoed the voice of Latin America, its thirst for freedom and independence, and its demand for respect from a domineering and arrogant power whose expansion was violating the rights of other nations. It was the voice of Bolívar and Santander, of Juárez and Martí, and of José Ingenieros (Argentine psychologist and sociologist, 1877–1925), who said in Buenos Aires in October, 1922, just at the time the United States was seeking to "Pan-Americanize" the Monroe Doctrine:

We are not, we no longer wish to be, we could not continue to be Pan-Americanists. . . . If the Monroe Doctrine might conceivably have been a guarantee during the past century of the "principle of nationalities" against the "right of intervention," it is evident today that that Doctrine . . . sets forth the "right of intervention" of the United States as against the Latin-American "principle of nationalities." A hypothetical guarantee was turned into a present danger. . . . That equivocal Doctrine, which never managed to be applied against European interventions, has had the function, finally, of assuring the exclusiveness of United States interventions. . . . This is what recent United States imperialist policy which has followed an alarming course for all Latin America, suggests to us.[31]

And after recalling Max Henríquez Ureña's characterization of the "general system of conquest" employed by the United States, Ingenieros added in a remarkably timely passage:

These words contain a serious warning—danger does not start with annexation, as in Puerto Rico; nor with intervention, as in Cuba; nor with a military expedition, as in Mexico; nor with armed occupation, as in Haiti; nor with purchase, as in the Guianas. In its initial phase, the danger begins with the progressive mortgaging of national independence through loans intended to be renewed and increased indefinitely under increasingly more onerous conditions for the sovereignty of the "borrower." A long time ago, the Cuban apostle, José Martí, warned about what the eminent Enrique José Varona repeats so movingly today, "Let us beware lest the cooperation of powerful friends be transformed into a protectorate which is a bridge to servitude. . . ."

We believe that our peoples face an inexorable dilemma: either submissive surrender and praise of the Pan-American Union (America for the North Americans), or joining together to prepare to defend their independence by laying the foundations of a Latin-American Union (Latin America for the Latin Americans). We are aware that the latter task is a long and difficult one . . . but to be discouraged beforehand by its magnitude is tantamount to surrender.[32]

Notes

[1] R. A. Martínez, *op. cit.*, p. 153.
[2] *Bases and Empire*, by George Marion, New York, 1948, p 52.
[3] *Historia Económica de Cuba*, by Julio Le Riverend, Havana, 1963, p. 202.
[4] *Ibid.*, pp. 206–207.
[5] *Our Cuban Colony*, by Leland W. Jenks, New York, 1928, p. 80.
[6] *Ibid.*
[7] *El Universo en Martí*, Ministerio de Relaciones Exteriores de Cuba.

[8] *Obras Completas de Simón Bolívar*, Vol. II p. 260; R. A. Martínez, *op. cit.*, p. 153.

[9] George Marion, *op cit.*, p. 85.

[10] *Estructura Económica de Panama*, by David M. Turner, Mexico, 1958, pp. 58–59.

[11] *Ibid.*, p. 60.

[12] *Ibid.*, p. 66.

[13] Nearing and Freeman, *op. cit.*, pp. 81–82.

[14] *Ibid.*, p. 82.

[15] *Puerto Rico: Freedom and Power in the Caribbean*, by Gordon K. Lewis, Monthly Review Press, New York, 1963, p. 78.

[16] Isidro Fabela, *op. cit.*, pp. 198, 200.

[17] *Readings in American Foreign Policy*, edited by Robert A. Goldwin, Ralph Lerner, Gerald Stourah, New York, 1959, pp. 196–197.

[18] *A History of Latin America*, by George Pendle, London, 1963, p. 177.

[19] Isidro Fabela, *op. cit.*, pp. 149, 150.

[20] Lloyd Mecham, *op. cit.* p. 72.

[21] Gordon K. Lewis, *op. cit.*, p. 78.

[22] *Las primeras agresiones del imperialismo contra Venezuela*, by Eduardo Machado, Mexico, 1957, pp. 30–31.

[23] *La Política de Estados Unidos en América Latina (1913–1916)*, by Arthur S. Link, Mexico, 1960, p. 8.

[24] *Ibid.*, p. 15.

[25] *Minutes of the Conference*, Washington, 1915, pp. 116–17.

[26] Nearing and Freeman, *op. cit.*, p. 106.

[27] Oscar Waiss, *op. cit.*, pp. 23–24.

[28] *American Imperialism*, New York, 1951, p. 12.

[29] Arthur S. Link, *op. cit.*, p. 220.

[30] "La Doctrina Monroe y su Evolución" by Roque Sáenz Peña, in *Hispanoamérica en Lucha por su Independencia*, Mexico, 1962, pp. 181–207.

[31] "Por la Unión Latinoamericana" by José Ingenieros, in *Hispanoamérica en Lucha por su Independencia*, pp. 215–224.

[32] *Ibid.*

5. *The Gay Twenties*

The First World War had decisive consequences for the United States. While Germany came out of the conflict defeated militarily and bankrupt, and while England and France were seriously weakened after four long years of a war which took a high toll in material resources and human lives, the United States emerged triumphant and strengthened, transformed into a great power, and the new center-to-be of world economy. A few years of rapid growth sufficed to make the United States a big international creditor—a factor which in itself was to exercise mounting influence on the economic and political relations of the American continents.

Perhaps the most characteristic feature of the period was the massive flow of foreign capital, especially from the United States, into the main Latin-American countries whose economies thereby became more dependent and underdeveloped. As for the inter-American system, it once more became evident —at the 1923 meeting in Santiago, Chile, and with even greater clarity at the meeting held in Havana in 1928—that Latin America intended to close the door to constant foreign intervention which, in fact, was taking place in violation of the laws of every country and of the principle of self-determination of nations.

Foreign investments (not including isolated loans to Latin American countries which from the first decades of the twentieth century were mainly from Europe and almost always incredibly onerous) started to pour in during the 1870's and 1880's. They increased considerably between 1890 and 1914, and it was from that time on, in particular, that the flow reached extreme proportions. England, which had been first in the field, was soon displaced by the United States.

British investment in Latin America amounted to £86 million in 1870, increased to £150 million in 1885, and reached £757 million in 1913.[1] According to other estimates, British investments in Latin-American securities jumped from £425.7 to alomst £1.2 billion (calculated at face value and not issue price) between 1890 and 1928.

Direct as well as portfolio investments by the United States, which amounted to only $304.3 million in 1897, had already passed the $1 billion mark by 1908, and rose to $1.64 billion in 1914 and to $5.37 billion in 1929. A breakdown of the figures shows the following trends:

1. Generally speaking, direct investments were always the principal ones—those aimed at control of property, raw material production, and various services. However, while credits or security investments scarcely increased between 1908 and 1919, they soared from $418.1 million to $1.73 billion between 1919 and 1929.

2. Changes in geographical distribution were very significant. In 1897, Mexico and Central America absorbed 72.8 percent of United States investments; the Caribbean countries followed with 14.8 percent, and South America came last with 12.4 percent of the total. By 1914, although Mexico and Central America still led, their share had dropped to 57.7 percent and South America had moved into second place. In 1929, South America was firmly in first place with 56.2 percent of all United States investments, Mexico and Central America had dropped to second place with 23.5 percent, and the Caribbean countries to third place with 20.3 percent.

3. Important changes also took place in the allocation of investments:

(a) Mining and smelting which had absorbed 26 percent of investments in 1897, rose to 43.3 percent in 1914, and dropped to only 20.1 percent in 1929.

(b) Railroads, which initially absorbed 42.6 percent of total United States investments, took up only 14.7 percent as early as 1908, and declined steadily to 6.3 percent in 1929.

(c) Oil, however, which absorbed only 3.5 percent of investments at the beginning of the period, increased its share to 10.2 percent by 1914, and to 20.1 percent by 1929.

(d) In summary, United States investments in Latin America in 1897 went into railroads, mining, agriculture, and trade, in that order of importance. In the decade 1908–1919, mining was the main area of operation, but by 1929 it had moved into second place, behind agriculture, followed by oil, public services, and manufactures.

4. With regard to distribution by countries, in 1897 Mexico and Cuba were almost the sole recipients of direct investments from the United States. In 1929, Cuba took first place with $887 million, Mexico was in second place with $709.2 million, followed by Chile with $448.4 million, Venezuela with $356.7 million, and Peru with $161.5 million.

5. Finally, while the first United States investments in Latin America were made directly in each country and went mainly into railroads and mines, those of the 1920's were in large measure transacted through United States stock exchanges and went increasingly into infrastructure "financed with foreign resources whose objective was to develop external sector rather than internal sector economic activities."[2]

The twenties were anything but gay in Latin America. They were not, as in the United States, years of rapid economic growth, of incongruous and scandalous orgies under prohibition, of short-lived economic stability—the heyday of the movies, the Charleston, and the stock market. They were difficult years of foreign interventions, tyrannical governments, growing production for the foreign market, unfavorable terms of trade, and an increasing inflow of foreign capital which entered neither to industrialize nor to modernize the Latin-American economy, but rather to subordinate and bind it more and more to imperialist domination from the north.

Some progress was achieved by Latin America between the

First World War and the 1929 crash. Two or three countries made headway in their efforts toward industrialization. In others, a weak and nascent bourgeoisie came to power which, although gradually displacing the old landowning oligarchies or relegating them to secondary positions, were at the same time incorporated into activities in which the influence of foreign capital was becoming greater all the time.

Perhaps the most serious problem confronting Latin America during the twenties was that of foreign intervention, with all its well-known and lamentable consequences.

Although soft words with a Wilsonian ring were often repeated, seeming to herald a change in the Latin-American policy of the United States, in practice they were always accompanied by the Rooseveltian menace of the Big Stick. Interventionist zeal was evident everywhere and produced not only illegal aggressions but frankly criminal ones.

In 1922, for example, the following appeared in the *Chicago Tribune:* "We do not wish to anticipate the future, but everything leads us to surmise that sooner or later Mexico will bow to our sovereignty. If we cared to be prophetic, we would say that the nations to the south will feel our attraction by virtue of the law of political gravity. Penetration and absorption could be gradual or union might be born out of a crisis. A country like Mexico cannot remain in a state of economic stagnation and of social and political chaos."[3]

Such was the temper of those times. In 1922, Latin America shuddered at the massacre of Bolivian workers which accompanied the entry of foreign capital into the tin mines. Two years later, when Anaconda Copper acquired the rich Chuquicamata mine, violence flared in labor-management relations in Chile, too, and fraudulent practices against the treasury multiplied.[4]

The inflow of United States capital during the twenties could not even remotely be called a smooth process. Investors who were trying to crush the labor movement in the United States at the time were even more reactionary and violent in

Latin America. Whenever they deemed it necessary, they brought in the Marines to "establish order" by force: conclusive proofs were the armed aggressions in Nicaragua, Haiti, and Santo Domingo.

Recalling the role played by companies like United Fruit in Honduras, Guatemala, El Salvador, and other countries of Central America and the Caribbean, two North American authors wrote: "This powerful company crushed competitors, subjugated governments, controlled railway enterprises, ruined planters, strangled cooperatives, exploited workers, fought organized labor, and abused the consumers. This use of power by one company of a heavily industrialized nation in relatively weak foreign countries constitutes a clear type of economic imperialism."[5]

The attempt to strengthen the inter-American system could hardly be expected to make progress within the framework of such imperialism. In 1923, while abuses were being perpetrated over and over again on the Latin-American countries, the fifth Pan-American Conference took place in Santiago, Chile and, once more, all burning issues were pushed aside. The Conference accomplished little for good or ill and the problem of aliens was turned over to a meeting of jurists planned for the near future.

The meeting of a Committee of Jurists in Rio de Janeiro in 1927 realized an old Latin-American dream. The so-called right of intervention was rejected and condemned and when an international law code was being drafted, the delegate from Costa Rica, Luis Anderson, proposed that it provide that "no state may intervene in the internal affairs of another state." Commenting on the various proposals, Professor Yepes of Colombia said: "The patriotic anguish of certain American countries confronted with the prospect of more or less veiled interventions by other powers had to be felt in order to appreciate the importance of this article."[6]

At the sixth Pan-American Conference in Havana at the beginning of 1928, the topic of intervention was again discussed, but in an entirely different atmosphere. The principle of nonintervention had been unanimously accepted in Rio a few months before, with particularly enthusiastic support for the Costa Rican delegate's proposal coming from Cuba and Peru. In Havana, on the other hand, under the watchful eye of the United States Secretary of State, Charles Evans Hughes, what had just been unanimously approved was now rejected. The delegate from El Salvador firmly defended the principle of equality before the law among nations and— despite the new and disconcerting opposition of Cuba and Peru—proposed the adoption of a resolution which would clearly provide that "no state has the right to intervene in the internal affairs of another state." However, this resolution was not approved, despite the support of several Latin-American delegations.

The Latin-American countries were again divided and imperialism once more achieved its purpose. Barcia Trelles was to say very justly: "A large part of the responsibility for the things that happen . . . in the Hispanic-American world, undoubtedly lies in the north; but if it is true that the initiative comes from the north, it is also true that it finds fertile ground south of the Rio Grande. Hispanic America must reflect upon herself . . . must rid herself of complacency and realize that the sickness dwells within her own entrails."[7]

Notes

[1] These and the following figures are taken from a study by the UN's Economic Commission for Latin America (ECLA), *El Financiamiento Externo de América Latina,* New York, 1964, pp. 5–22.

[2] ECLA, *op. cit.,* p. 22.

[3] *La Política exterior norteamericana,* by C. Barcia Trelles, p. 25.

[4] *Las inversiones extranjeras in América Latina,* by Carlos Montenegro, Buenos Aires, 1962, p. 69.

[5] *El Imperio del Banano,* by C. D. Kepner, Jr. and J. H. Soothill, Buenos Aires, 1957, p. 31.

[6] Isidro Fabela, *op. cit.,* p. 206.

[7] *La doctrina de Monroe y la cooperación,* p. 737.

6. Depression and War

The world crisis which struck in the fall of 1929 was catastrophic. Not only did prices of goods and services and the stock market come crashing down, but illusions of indefinitely prolonged stability and prosperity tumbled with them. The economic boom that so many had enthusiastically proclaimed until the very eve of the crash was replaced by hunger, misery, and unemployment. The unexpected upheaval shook nations, big and small, and from the ruins emerged Nazism and the discontent of people wanting bread, work, progress, freedom, and independence.

The chaos produced by the crisis was unprecedented. Production in capitalist countries underwent an amazing slump, dropping overall to the 1908–09 level. The decline in industrial production, in particular, was disastrous: 23.8 percent in England, 32.9 percent in France, 40.6 percent in Germany, and 46.2 percent in the United States. Coal and steel production in the United States regressed 28 and 31 years, respectively, while iron output and shipbuilding in England dropped to the levels of 71 and 90 years before.[1]

Between 1929 and 1932, national income in the United States dropped from $81 billion to $40 billion; rural income was reduced to less than half; and wages in the principal sectors, including mining and manufacturing, fell from over $17 billion to $7.2 billion. The employment index (base: 1923–25=100) fell from 106 to 66, and the total value of exports and imports fell from $9.6 billion to $2.9 billion.[2]

Popular discontent under such conditions appeared quickly. Workers protested vociferously against unemployment and low wages; everywhere farmers became more indignant at the

67

ridiculous prices being paid for their products; unemployment and misery increased even in countries which had been boasting a few months before of their permanent prosperity. Social and economic contradictions deepened and their solution seemed less and less possible; hunger spread while flour, cereals, fruits, and other foods were being burned, destroyed, or dumped into the sea in many places; and Fascist armies marched, arrogantly leaving the first trails of blood and oppression in their wake.

The struggle of all the peoples, first against depression and unemployment and soon after against Fascism, aggression, and the imminent danger of another war, had a decisive effect on United States policy in Latin America as well as on the scope and orientation of Pan-Americanism.

The primary concern of the United States between 1910 and 1930 had been to protect her investors, particularly in those areas she considered under her influence. As late as 1927, President Coolidge was still declaring, "The person and property of a citizen are part of the general domain of the Nation, even when abroad."[3] And this same thesis, in violation of national sovereignty, would be put forward again in Havana the following year. Addressing the sixth Pan-American Conference, the United States delegate, Hughes, asserted that when a government could not provide proper protection, "under such circumstances another government has the right, I will not say to intervene, but to interpose in a temporary manner to protect the lives and interests of its nationals."[4] This, in essence, was the so-called Evart Doctrine, a "doctrine dug up by Mr. Coolidge by which the protection of United States money invested in foreign countries becomes a supreme obligation of the government in Washington, above even respect for the freedom of an autonomous country and the independence of sovereign states."[5]

Beginning with the Hoover Administration, however, United States policy in Latin America began to undergo a change as a result of the situation prevailing throughout the world. The "corollary" to the Monroe Doctrine introduced by Theodore Roosevelt some years earlier was beginning to be relinquished; the position of the Wilson Administration, in favor of exclusive recognition of *de jure* governments, was abandoned; United States Marines were withdrawn from Nicaragua and the State Department warned United States investors that in case of conflict they should exhaust the possibilities of solution within the country in which they had invested before appealing to their own governments.

The principal changes took place during the Administration of Franklin D. Roosevelt, within the framework of what he called the "Good Neighbor Policy," by which he hoped to create "an atmosphere of close understanding and cooperation," and to insure "respect for the rights of others and a scrupulous fulfillment of the corresponding obligations by each member of the community."

Of course, the Good Neighbor Policy was not precisely what many people desired or supposed it to be—the end of imperialism—but neither was it merely an empty phrase. It was a step forward as far as the aggressive behavior of the United States was concerned, behavior which had culminated in armed interventions in Mexico, Central America, and the Caribbean. It also constituted a victory for the democratic forces of the continent.

Roosevelt's policy did not succeed in modifying the monopolistic structure of the United States economy, nor in a deeper sense, did it seek to do so. Neither did it affect the very basis of United States—Latin-American relations. The countries south of the Rio Grande remained subjugated to the great power in the north and very soon the illusion vanished that things would change radically.

The people generally hoped that the Good Neighbor Policy might mean an end to colonial exploitation. They had hoped for assistance, without conditions, for industrialization; they had hoped for effective cooperation to get out of the crisis. "However, as the new policy was applied it became increasingly clear that while it had important positive features, the basic character of imperialist domination prevailed."[6]

Referring to the Good Neighbor Policy some years later, the Mexican economist Jesús Silva Herzog said:

> It is impossible to deny Roosevelt's international achievements. In relation to the Latin-American countries it has meant . . . a change from the past. The big stick has been replaced by the white glove; [but] compared with the policy of the other Roosevelt, the Good Neighbor Policy is a change of form rather than content. . . . Imperialism, an economic phenomenon, inevitable and legitimate offspring of capitalism, will never cease to be a constant threat and a growing evil for the progress . . . of the majority of nations, until capitalist society transforms itself into a new society capable of superseding the bloody civilizations of the merchant.[7]

The Good Neighbor Policy, because of its very nature, contained insoluble contradictions. While, on the one hand, it showed respect, previously nonexistent, for the Latin-American nations, on the other hand, it manifested itself as an effort to further subordinate them to United States economic needs. Even Roosevelt himself believed in the advantage of increasing investments in Latin America "in order to develop sources of raw materials needed in the United States."[8]

Nevertheless, in 1933 the United States recognized the principle of legal equality among nations, the principle of non-intervention in the domestic or foreign affairs of another country, the principle of territorial integrity, and the need to outlaw the use of force in international relations. The fruit of this progress was reaped in the years that followed. The United States ended the occupation of Haiti; an agreement was signed with Panama; the Platt Amendment was abolished and a new reciprocal trade treaty signed with Cuba; certain social and economic reforms were accepted, albeit reluctantly, by the United States, as well as protectionist measures which she had previously obstinately opposed; and her attitude concerning her investors abroad was considerably modified. After all the years of the Stars and Stripes following the dollar, in 1935 the Assistant Secretary of State, Sumner Welles declared, "It is my belief that American capital invested abroad, in fact as well as in theory, should be subordinated to the authority of the people of the country where it is located."⁹

With favorable changes taking place in America despite many old unresolved problems, a promising outlook for improved inter-American relations seemed to be in view. In Europe, however, the panorama was darkening and the growth of Fascism was creating a situation whose consequences were soon to affect the American continents.

In 1933, the seventh Pan-American Conference was held in Montevideo where, after years of unsuccessful efforts, the following resolution was finally adopted: "No state has the right to interfere in the internal or external affairs of another state." Speaking for the United States, Secretary of State Cordell Hull said, "Under the Administration of President Roosevelt, the government of the United States is opposed, as much as any other government is opposed, to any interference in the liberty, sovereignty or domestic affairs or procedures of the governments of other nations."¹⁰

The acceptance of the principle of nonintervention by the United States, which had systematically and emphatically rejected it up to then, provoked a wave of optimism and a brief period of euphoria in Latin America. But while the United States continued to interfere in Latin-American affairs in one way or another, as in the Chaco War between Paraguay and Bolivia in 1932–1935 (for possession of a territory of 20,000 square miles—won by Paraguay) and in other instances, it maintained a paradoxically noninterventionist position toward Fascist aggression, which meant loss of freedom and violation of territorial integrity for Spain, Ethiopia, Czechoslovakia, and other nations.

The "nonintervention" policy toward Fascism was a way of intervening on its behalf. As President Lázaro Cárdenas of Mexico correctly expressed it at the time: "The term 'nonintervention' is a screen being used by certain nations in order

to deny aid to the legally constituted Spanish government.
Mexico cannot share in this criterion inasmuch as non-coopera-
tion with the constitutional authorities of a friendly nation
is, in practice, indirect aid—and no less effective for that reason—to the rebels threatening the regime which those authorities represent. Therefore, such nonintervention is in itself one
of the most cautious ways of intervening."[11]

Until 1935, the inter-American system had revolved around
more or less concrete problems in which it was generally easy
to recognize the conflict of interests between Latin America
and the United States. As the international situation deterio-
rated and Nazi-Fascist aggression advanced unchecked by the
League of Nations, impotent to preserve peace, the danger of
a new war became of increasing concern. In December, 1936,
on President Roosevelt's initiative, the Inter-American Conference for the Maintenance of Peace was held in Buenos
Aires. In his significant message to the meeting, Roosevelt
said:

> We know, too, that vast armaments are rising on every side.
> . . . We know that Nations guilty of these follies inevitably face
> the day when either their weapons of destruction must be used
> against their neighbors or when an unsound economy, like a
> house of cards, will fall apart. . . .
> It is no accident that, because of these suicidal policies and
> the suffering attending them, many of their people have come
> to believe with despair that the price of war seems less than the
> price of peace. . . .
> Sacrifices in the cause of peace are infinitesimal compared
> with the holocaust of war.[12]

In the same message, President Roosevelt spoke of the
need to defend "representative democracy" and of his faith in
that type of government as the best instrument for insuring
the social, economic, and cultural development of a just and
peaceful world. His reference to a democratic system was
important because after the resolutions of the Buenos Aires
conference, the defense of democracy against Fascism was to
be given increased attention.

From the opening of the 1936 meeting, both Roosevelt and Hull stressed the need for establishing a system of defense against possible extracontinental aggressions. Hull even proposed the formation of a permanent inter-American consultative committee. Argentina objected to the proposal on the ground that if it were accepted, America would be segregated from the jurisdiction of the League of Nations, thereby weakening world organization. Objections were also raised against the policy of neutrality suggested by the United States in case of war. But in the end a pact was signed which provided for consultation among American countries if the peace of the continent should be threatened. Although the proposed mechanism for consultation was never formally established and the United States abandoned its original idea of a mutual defense pact, the Buenos Aires agreement represented the beginning of a new phase in the life of the inter-American system since the possibility of collective action against the eventuality of foreign threats was accepted for the first time.

The course initiated in Buenos Aires was more clearly defined in Lima two years later. In 1938, war seemed imminent: the victims of Nazism increased and the Munich Pact, presented by Chamberlain and Daladier as a triumph of Anglo-French diplomacy, instead of lessening the danger of war, made it more acute than ever. It was against such a background that the eighth Pan-American Conference was held in Lima, at which Roosevelt proposed "a defensive alliance for the American nations against outside aggression."

Mounting United States pressure provoked understandable suspicion and reservations. Nobody could deny the increasing danger of Nazi aggression. However, the Latin countries feared that a defense pact with the United States as the hub would open the door to constantly expanding U.S. penetration into their affairs and to a dangerous and unacceptable subordination on their part. Some countries were opposed to such a pact for this reason and other countries were opposed for other reasons —Argentina, for example, had close relations with Italy and

Germany. All agreed, however, to a declaration which affirmed American solidarity and the intention of defending it, created a consultative mechanism, and provided—also, for the first time—for common action against subversive activities. At the same time, in the face of the fears and reservations of various countries, it was clearly defined that "the governments of the American republics would act independently in the exercise of their national sovereignty."

Other important agreements were reached at the conference. The so-called Lima Declaration ratified the nonintervention protocol approved in Buenos Aires and the principle of "continental solidarity" was reiterated, establishing that the governments of America, "faithful to the principles already stated and to their absolute sovereignty, reaffirm their decision to maintain and defend them against any outside intervention or activity that might threaten them."

The following additional principles were included in the declaration, obviously as a response to Fascism: (1) The inadmissibility of intervention in the internal or external affairs of one state by another; (2) the peaceful settlement of all international disputes; and (3) the outlawing of force as an instrument of national or international policy.[13]

On ratifying the Lima Declaration, the Mexican delegate, Manuel J. Sierra, observed that "the main goal of continental action in favor of peace should not only be the peaceful solution of international conflicts . . . but also the elimination of the causes giving rise to them." He also expressed his conviction that the consultative system would uphold and maintain the principles of nonintervention consecrated in 1933 and 1936. On the bases of these principles, the Mexican delegation made three proposals: (1) "Relinquishment by aliens of the diplomatic protection of their own governments"; (2) "restriction of the use of force in collecting contractual debts"; and (3) "extinctive prescription of international obligations." These were turned over to other bodies for study and consequently did not come up as resolutions.[14]

The Lima Conference was important. It became evident there that the United States was concerned about the threat of war and was counting on Latin America in such a contingency. The old Monroe Doctrine bloomed anew in Lima, its expansionist character coming to the fore once again and although its unilateral nature remained unchanged, a significant modification did undoubtedly appear. "What has taken place," commented Sumner Welles, "is not a change of policy, but a change in emphasis. The emphasis is now on joint action rather than on single action."[15]

World War II had just begun when the first Consultative Meeting of American Foreign Ministers was held in September, 1939. The Buenos Aires and Lima Declarations were reaffirmed and fervent hopes were expressed for the end of the war in Europe. Upon the motion of the Mexican delegate, General Eduardo Hay, it was established that "each country was free to approve the agreements [of the meeting of ministers] in accordance with its laws" or, as had been provided at Lima, solidarity would be made operative by "the coordination of the respective sovereign wills" of the countries, acting "independently in their individual capacities, [and] fully recognizing their legal equality as sovereign states."[16]

Speaking to the Council of the Pan-American Union on April 14, 1939, President Roosevelt stated: "The issue is really whether our civilization is to be dragged into the tragic vortex of unlimited militarism, punctuated by periodic wars. . . . We have the right to say that there shall not be an organization of world affairs which permits us no choice but to turn our countries into barracks, unless we are to be the vassals of some conquering empire."[17]

In 1940, the war continued spreading and the danger that America would be involved became more serious. In another message, whose principal interest perhaps lay in its recognition of the tragic consequences of a policy of appeasement of

Fascism, Roosevelt said: "It can no longer be disputed that forces of evil which are bent on conquest of the world will destroy whomever they can whenever they can. We know now that if we seek to appease them . . . we only hasten the day of their attack upon us."[18]

In accordance with this conviction, the second Consultative Meeting of American Foreign Ministers was held in Havana in 1940, where the following declaration was made: "Any attack by a non-American state on the integrity or territorial inviolability of an American state or against its sovereignty or political independence, will be considered an act of aggression against the states signing this declaration," and it was further pointed out that in such an event "the signatory states will consult among themselves to determine what measure should be taken."

In June, 1941, after overrunning Europe from France to Poland, Germany attacked the Soviet Union. A few months later, Japan, also without a previous declaration of war, bombed Pearl Harbor, which turned the conflict into an unprecedented world conflagration. A few months after the United States was dragged into the war, the third Consultative Meeting was held in Rio de Janeiro. Its importance was more symbolic than anything else inasmuch as it reaffirmed previously adopted principles, such as solidarity and nonintervention. Thereby, two not readily reconcilable interests once again came to the fore. On the one hand, the United States was counting on Latin America; and, on the other, Latin America was afraid of compromising its national sovereignty by possible forms of intervention or subordination to United States war strategy.

The Second World War had a contradictory effect on the countries of Latin America. The closing of foreign markets momentarily increased their supply problems but as the conflict dragged on, endowed with extensive resources and favored by other circumstances, they began to make progress toward the diversification of their economies. The decade prior to the war had been especially difficult; the contraction of the economy brought about by a sharp drop in exports and the sudden paralysis of international movements of capital produced increasing balance of payments deficits, suspension of foreign debt services and the breakdown of credit systems. After the conflict began, the panorama started to change and Latin America was soon able to accumulate considerable foreign exchange reserves. For the first time in a very long while, Latin-American countries also found themselves having a certain freedom of action vis-à-vis the big trusts. Furthermore, the inability of the industrial countries to supply the world market enabled the Latin-American countries to produce goods which they had previously imported and they were even able to export merchandise traditionally supplied them by the industrialized countries.

During the war, new industries were born, and many of the existing ones consolidated their positions and gained ground. But Latin America did not cease being primarily a raw material producing and exporting region, although it did succeed in achieving certain advances which modified its economic structure. However, the benefits of this transformation, particularly the most immediate ones, were concentrated among small privileged national and foreign groups, because the severe inflation which, in fact, existed from the first day of the war, served as an effective instrument for the distribution and transferral of income in favor of the rich and to the detriment of the general population.

The war strengthened United States interests in Latin America and in particular weakened resistance against imperialism. In many cases, the policy of "national unity" meant temporizing and regressing; it also encouraged those opportunists who recognized the necessity of carrying on the struggle against Nazism but at the same time did not seem to have a clear awareness of the equally fundamental necessities of protecting national sovereignty against imperialist incursion, and of laying the foundations of independent economic development.

During the war years, U.S. capital flowed on a larger scale than in the previous decade. It was quite plain that the United States intended to help explore and exploit the productive resources of Latin America in order to achieve a certain measure of economic integration and to make the Latin-American economy more complimentary to its own. According to Mecham, this explains why many of the activities promoted by the United States may have been "integral and essential features of the hemisphere defense structure."[19]

Until the end of the thirties, inter-American cooperation was chiefly economic and cultural. With the rise of the Nazi-Fascist threat in Europe, the emphasis changed. Military defense suddenly took on a new priority. From that time on, the principal objectives of United States policy would be: (1) to eliminate the threat in the Western Hemisphere of Nazi subversion; (2) to utilize the military potential of Latin America to the utmost in primarily defensive roles; (3) to be able to count on naval and air bases in Latin-American countries; (4) to maintain a stable political situation there and a sympathetic attitude toward United States policy; and (5) to assure full access to Latin-American strategic raw materials.[20]

From the outset of the war, in line with these aims the United States began to supersede German and Italian military missions in Latin America; organized training courses for foreign officers; agreed to sell war matériel to Latin America at cost; and, on its own initiative, created the Inter-American Political Defense Commission for dealing with the danger of internal subversion, as well as the Inter-American Defense Board, which was made a permanent organization at the Chapultepec Conference (1945) and was at the service, in fact, of United States military policy.

In spite of all this, the United States position during World War II had its positive aspects. Until the death of Roosevelt, it was on the side of democracy and liberty and opposed to Fascism, and it contributed in large measure to liberating humanity from Nazi oppression and Hitler's dream of a thousand years of German domination. In those days, United States policy was one of respect for domestic democratic guarantees as well as for the sovereignty of other nations. Important reforms were achieved under President Roosevelt's Administration, corruption was fought, opposition to monopolies organized, democratic traditions re-established, and the popular struggle against Fascism encouraged. Thus, Roosevelt was right in stating in a speech delivered at the beginning of 1944: "If history were to repeat itself and we were to return to the so-called normalcy of the 1920's—then it is certain that even though we shall have conquered our enemies on the battlefields abroad, we shall have yielded to the spirit of Fascism here at home."

Notes

[1] *La crisis general del capitalismo*, by M. Draguilev, Moscow, 1960, p. 101.
[2] *We, the People*, by Leo Huberman, pp. 260–262.
[3] *U.S. Over Latin America*, by Herman Olden, New York, 1955, p. 7.
[4] *The New York Times*, February 19, 1928.
[5] *Los Estados Unidos y la América Latina (1921–1929)* by Isidro Fabela, Mexico, 1955.
[6] H. Olden, *op. cit.*, p. 9.
[7] *"Imperialismo y buena vecindad"* (Mesa Rodante), in *Cuadernos Americanos*, Mexico, Sept.–Oct., 1947, p. 67.
[8] *The Great Fear*, by John Gerassi, New York, 1963, p. 220.
[9] *Ibid.*, p. 219.
[10] *Intervención*, by Isidro Fabela, p. 217.
[11] *Cartas al Presidente Cárdenas*, by Isidro Fabela, Mexico, 1947, p. 8.
[12] *Nothing to Fear, The Selected Addresses of F. D. Roosevelt, 1932–1945*, New York, 1946, pp. 606–608.
[13] *Intervención*, by Isidro Fabela, pp. 232–233.
[14] *Ibid.*, pp. 233–241.
[15] *Your Foreign Policy*, by Robert A. Smith, New York, 1941, pp. 200–201.
[16] Isidro Fabela, *op. cit.*, pp. 295–296.
[17] *The Public Papers and Addresses of FDR*, New York, 1941, Vol. 8, p. 199.
[18] *Ibid.*, Vol. 9, p. 466.
[19] L. Mecham, *op. cit.*, p. 205.
[20] *Arms and Politics in Latin America*, by Edwin Lieuwen, New York, 1960.

7. The Eve of a Third World War

Franklin Delano Roosevelt's death grieved the world. For over a decade, he had been an outstanding political figure and one of the "greats" of the world in the struggle against Nazi barbarism, and his presence had evoked friendliness everywhere. Harry S. Truman, his successor, sounded like Roosevelt when, on assuming the presidency, he said that "division in the United Nations must be avoided" and provocations should be guarded against. But within a few days, Roosevelt's policies began to be abandoned, countered, and betrayed.

This change inside the United States could not avoid having repercussions abroad. The days of the New Deal and the Good Neighbor Policy were over. The old Monroe Doctrine came to the fore again, but with a new name and physiognomy. Henceforth, it was to be called the Truman Doctrine, and its principal international objectives would be: To bring pressure on the Soviet Union and obstruct its reconstruction; to back the reactionary regimes of Greece and Turkey and all countries where such regimes were about to collapse; to maintain the *status quo* in those European nations whose peoples were struggling to bring about democratic changes; to gain ground in the competition against England and France; to extend United States domination in the Middle East, Africa, Asia, and Latin America; to weaken the United Nations; and to replace the policy of conciliation and peaceful negotiation with one of force. The United States was to employ the Marshall Plan in Europe and the Inter-American System in Latin America as its main instruments.

After 1945, it was clear that the course of the international situation would not run favorably for Latin America. At the 1945 Chapultepec Conference, a special meeting of Ministers of Foreign Affairs called to discuss problems of war and peace, the United States delegation, headed by Secretary of State Stettinius and including William Clayton, brought pressure to bear to obtain greater military cooperation and increased dependence. While the countries south of the Rio Grande hoped to consolidate the modest industrial development they had achieved during the war—thanks to a protectionist and developmental policy, to the temporary withdrawal of the great powers from their traditional markets, and to better trade relations—the United States appeared at the conference with the so-called Clayton Plan. Under this plan, the United States tried to push through the thesis of unrestricted freedom of trade which signified a return to the "normalcy" of the past; that is to say, to a situation whereby the great industrial countries, especially the United States, would recapture their old markets and expand their influence everywhere. In 1947, at a preliminary meeting held in Geneva, and afterward at the United Nations World Conference on Trade and Employment held in Havana, the anachronistic ideas previously propounded by William Clayton were pushed to the fore and adopted in the "Havana Charter." Again, freedom of trade and protectionist measures were brought up and again there was a clash between the poor countries eager to industrialize and the self-assured powers, aware that this "freedom" they were demanding meant indefinite servitude for the economically backward nations.

As Clayton himself would say, the policy supported in Havana was the most advantageous one for his country. He pointed out that "the productive capacity of the United States in the area of industry is equivalent to that of the rest of the world combined. We need to import all sorts of raw materials from everywhere to feed our huge production machine. . . . We have much to gain and nothing to lose by large-scale development of the exchange of goods and services."[1] And Jesús

Reyes Heroles, a member of the Mexican delegation to the conference wrote:

> The Havana Charter turns out to mean no more than the following: Through this document, the highly developed countries are assured of supplies of the raw materials and natural resources of the world under internationally secured conditions; they are assured of the sale of their manufactures in the world markets, and . . . the disposal of their surplus capital in all the countries of the world, also under internationally secured conditions, is guaranteed. . . .
>
> Historically, the Charter amounts to no more than a document designed to perpetuate the economic *status quo* of the world . . . a document whereby the colonial countries obligate themselves never to take precisely those measures which are necessary to enable them to break out of their economic situation even though all the factors warranting the adoption of such measures would continue to exist.[2]

But most serious of all for Latin America was not what took place in Havana in 1947, but the agreements adopted at Rio de Janeiro the same year. Up to that time, the "Communist threat" had served to maintain international tension in order to justify open support of numerous anti-popular governments, to bury the New Deal, to keep open the armaments factories which were still a source of fat profits, and to strengthen the most conservative groups in the United States and other countries. However, despite all this, the possibility perhaps never occurred to anybody that a military pact—not one of peace and friendly cooperation—could be signed on the American continent right at the end of the war. It was naturally assumed by everybody that the military obligations and agreements of the war years would become obsolete since, obviously, they were no longer necessary. But hardly had the most devastating war ever borne by humanity come to an end than the United States made Latin America accept a military pact.

The Inter-American Reciprocal Assistance provided:

Article 2. . . . the High Contracting Parties undertake to submit every controversy which may arise among them to methods of peaceful settlement and to endeavor to settle any such controversy among themselves by means of the procedures in force in the inter-American System before referring it to the General Assembly or Security Council of the United Nations.

Article 3. The High Contracting Parties agree that an armed attack by any State against an American State shall be considered as an attack against all the American States, and, consequently, each one of the said Contracting Parties undertakes to assist in meeting the attack. . . .

Article 6. If the inviolability or integrity of the territory or the sovereignty or political independence of any American State should be affected by an aggression which is not an armed attack or by an extra-continental or intra-continental conflict or by any other fact or situation that might endanger the peace of America, the Organ of Consultation shall meet immediately in order to agree on the measures [appropriate in the case].

Article 8. . . . the measures on which the Organ of Consultation may agree will comprise one or more of the following: recall of chiefs of diplomatic missions; breaking of diplomatic . . . and consular relations; partial or complete interruption of economic relations or . . . communications; and the use of armed force.

Article 17. The Organ of Consultation shall take its decisions by a vote of two-thirds of the Signatory States which have ratified the Treaty.

Article 20. Decisions which require the application of the measure specified in Article 8 shall be binding upon all the signatory States . . . with the sole exception that no State shall be required to use armed force without its consent . . .[3]

The Rio de Janeiro Treaty modified the very foundation upon which Pan-Americanism had rested until then. Not even at the time of Blaine and "manifest destiny," during the time of Wilson and World War I, or throughout the years of struggle against Fascism was a decision with such grave implications reached as that adopted in Rio in 1947. The Inter-American Treaty of Reciprocal Assistance was not only the first military treaty signed in America in peacetime; it was also an instrument intended to undermine Latin-American sovereignty, to submit the most important national decisions to the vote of other countries, and to try to hold back the course of history by alleging that the advance of Socialist countries and of liberation movements was the worst threat to the world that had arisen out of the war. The United States attitude clearly revealed the inability of its governing classes to comprehend that the desire of the people for progress and change could not be sacrificed to privilege and vested interests, that the world would go forward without the wheels of history stopping, and that the breaking of ancient chains endangered nobody but those who placed their own selfish interests above mankind's noblest aspirations.

Lieuwen asserts that, as a result of the Rio Treaty, Latin America inevitably took a subordinate place in the newly developing global foreign policy of the United States.[4] This was inescapable from the moment Latin America acquiesced to the totally unjustified extension and amplification of the obligations assumed under the Act of Chapultepec, signed in Mexico in 1945. In fact, as Narciso Bassols (a leading Mexican jurist and political thinker) indicated so opportunely, while everybody at Chapultepec had agreed on the necessity of a united response against any "*act of aggression*" from any state, American or not, the Rio Treaty did not refer to "mere acts of aggression . . . but at one fell swoop, with a stroke of the pen . . . extended economic and military solidarity to cover any case of *armed attack* against an American state."[5]

> The Rio Treaty is a big step toward war . . . because it encourages the United States imperialist forces . . . since it hands over the cooperation of Latin America in whatever conflict they provoke; and, because, in violation of Article 53 of the San Francisco Charter, it constitutes a serious attack against the United Nations by establishing that any American country and, of course, all of them together, may carry out coercive military measures, that is to say, make war, without the authorization of the Security Council. In addition, by completely twisting the concepts of legitimate defense and "action of a regional nature,"

it also violates Articles 51 and 52 of the same San Francisco Charter.[6]

Recalling Truman's unfortunate statements to the effect that victory had imposed the responsibility of leading the world upon the people of the United States as a permanent burden, Bassols wrote:

> The Latin-American people support continental defense. But on a specific condition: that this idea should not be used to shield any sort of expansionist adventures on other continents, or struggles aimed at the violent conquest of world domination. . . . The gravest aspect of the alliance entered into in Rio de Janeiro . . . lies in that with one stroke of the pen, Latin-American countries are transformed into the compulsory, automatic allies of the United States . . . in whatever kind of war might break out from that day on. . . .
>
> In 1940, the threat of aggression hung over all the countries of the earth, because Hitler and his allies . . . were on the march toward violent domination of all the continents. Under those conditions, the creation of an inter-American defense mechanism was a sincere, natural step. There were aggressors. . . . Today, the situation is diametrically opposite, but inasmuch as the true objective cannot be admitted, nor is it convenient to discard the defensive phraseology which naturally arouses the sympathy of the masses, diplomatic juggling must be resorted to in order to transform a pact which was originally purely defensive into an instrument for the military and political unification of the whole continent.[7]

But the Rio accord had its price and the signing of it was received with a great deal less than enthusiasm. The United States began exerting pressure even prior to the Chapultepec conference to bolster "hemispheric defense" and did not let up after the war had ended. Toward the end of 1945, the United States Defense Board recommended "standardization of the organization and training of the armed forces" of the continent, and a few months later President Truman sent Congress the Inter-American Military Cooperation Bill in which the above recommendation was stressed.

The insistence of the United States upon the adoption of

military measures fostered a current of Latin-American opinion in favor of economic aid. Public officials and businessmen suggested that with its vast resources the United States should contribute to the development of their economies and that Latin America needed a Marshall Plan. These opinions began to gain strength in 1947, precisely at a time when social unrest was becoming acute in the Latin-American countries, when financial reserves painstakingly accumulated during the war had started to dwindle, industrial advance was endangered, inflation was intensified through the squandering of the wealthy, the devaluations, and the lack of a policy seriously concerned with attacking the principal causes of imbalance. Right at the Rio meeting, Jaime Torres Bodet, Mexico's Foreign Secretary, stated that political-military defense was only half the problem; the other half was the question of mutual aid for raising living standards. And he added that unless the same unity of action planned against political enemies was directed toward eradicating poverty, ignorance, and disease, the American nations could not be said to be getting at the core of the problem.[8]

It was understandable that Latin-American governing groups should think in terms of setting a cash price in exchange for military aid and, in particular, for the political solidarity the United States wanted. They were willing to join the new anti-Communist crusade but were quite frank about expecting to be well remunerated.

Notes

[1] Quoted in *La Carta de la Habana*, by Jesús Reyes Heroles, Mexico, 1948, p. 144.

[2] *Ibid.*, p. 143.

[3] Text of the Treaty. See *Readings in American Foreign Policy*, pp. 209–213.

[4] Edwin Lieuwen, *op. cit.*

[5] "¿Alianza automática? Desgracaciadamente, sí," by Narciso Bassols, *El Universal*, October 6, 1947.

[6] *Ibid.*

[7] *Obras*, by Narciso Bassols, Mexico, 1964.

[8] *The New York Times*, August 16, 1947.

8. From Bogotá to Caracas

The ninth Pan-American Conference held in Bogotá in 1948 was just as important as the Rio de Janeiro conference of the previous year. It reorganized the Pan-American system according to a threefold purpose: (1) To consider the Rio Treaty one of the main instruments of the system; (2) to withdraw inter-American relations, in fact, from the United Nations framework; and (3) to provide facilities for United States investors wishing to exploit the resources of Latin America.

Inasmuch as businessmen and even numerous government officials kept calling for a Marshall Plan for Latin America, the United States hastened to send General George Marshall himself as chairman of its delegation in charge of "marshallizing" Latin America. However, the General arrived in Bogotá with empty pockets. Instead of the millions he had distributed in Europe, all he offered Latin America was aid in combating Communism, and United States investments—as soon as a "favorable climate" was provided. Marshall's objective in Bogotá was essentially the same as that of the United States everywhere at the time: To halt the spread of socialism, to block it as a potential force, to oppose any basic changes, to invent an imminent danger to "Christian civilization," and to incorporate other countries into the overall anti-Communist strategy.

The Bogotá conference approved various important documents: The Charter of the Organization of American States, the Pact of Bogotá, an Economic Pact, a Charter of Social Guarantees, a Declaration of the Rights and Duties of Man, and numerous special resolutions on political, legal, economic, and military matters.

The principles incorporated in the Charter of the OAS were basically the same as those which had so often been reiterated since 1933. On his return from Bogotá, one of the Mexican delegates to the conference emphasized the following principles as being the most important: The equality of states; respect for their legal status; recognition of international law, treaties, and good faith as the norms of conduct; outlawing of the use of force; coordination with the UN; peaceful settlement of disputes; recognition of human rights; economic, social, and cultural cooperation; and solidarity against aggression.[1]

On the principle of nonintervention, in particular, not only were the decisions of previous meetings applied, but that principle was broadened to make inadmissible collective intervention, any form of interference besides armed intervention, and "any activity threatening the legal status of the state."[2] The first part of Article 15 of the Charter established that "No state or group of states has the right to intervene, directly or indirectly, for any reason, in the internal or external affairs of any other state." To counteract the frequent pressures brought to bear on them, the Latin-American countries managed to put through Article 16 which provided that "No state shall apply or encourage coercive economic or political measures for the purpose of violating the sovereign will or to take advantage of it in any way." One of the steps toward the attainment of the principles of the Charter, provided by Article 4, was: "To promote economic, social, and cultural development by means of cooperative action."

However, the framework within which the problems of development were set forth was mainly the traditional one: the United States seeking to regain its temporarily lost positions in certain fields and, at the same time, to consolidate and extend its influence in others. It continued to look upon Latin America as a storehouse of natural resources and raw materials, as a group of subordinate economies which should continue producing and exporting coffee, bananas, cereals, meat, copper, lead, and tin. While several of the Latin-American countries did make some feeble efforts to break up the old system of exploitation and dependence, this was done timidly and, as usual, on an individual basis.

In the long run, the Bogotá Economic Agreement failed to satisfy anyone fully. Unwarranted concessions were made in certain areas by various countries. And what finally remained was a more or less eclectic document which, although inordinately praised at times, did not really represent a serious and objective study of the problems of Latin-American development; nor could it serve as the basis of a proper plan of economic strategy. As a matter of fact, at the same time that Latin America indicated that industrialization must be promoted, prices for primary products raised, and mechanisms for efficient economic cooperation created, it also agreed to accept the kind of international trade that was and is a cause of its backwardness—as the UN's Economic Commission for Latin America (ECLA) kept pointing out from 1949 on— along with an approach to development which assigned a very important role to foreign capital.

Gilberto Loyo, one of the Mexican delegates, remarked about this agreement after the meeting was over: "Economic progress should be achieved through the stimulation of local investment of national savings and foreign capital. . . . The majority of the American states, being raw material producers . . . have a very limited capacity to accumulate national savings. In some cases, this insufficiency is aggravated by the inadequate utilization of those savings. . . . The states needing investments and those able to make them should provide each other with reciprocal opportunities and stimuli for investment and reinvestment without, under normal conditions, the imposition of unjustified restrictions, on the transfer of capital and profits from it."[3]

Another Mexican delegate to the Bogotá conference asserted that: "Practically unanimous consensus was achieved . . . that foreign investments, when given a proper orientation, can be a very important factor in accelerating development

. . . ; consensus has also been reached that no state shall take unreasonable action . . . which may infringe on the rights or interests of nationals or aliens, or with regard to the equitable treatment of foreign capital."[4]

In summary, despite the fact that many United States investors had undoubtedly hoped to obtain privileged treatment in Bogotá beyond that accorded even to the citizens of the particular country, what they did get was the offer of a system of guarantees and stimuli and the promise of equal treatment to that of nationals, which was to enable them to continue to extend their control in Latin America.

In other words, what the delegates did at Bogotá was to evade the basic problems. They refused to grapple with decisive obstacles to development and, for the most part, tied progress to United States financial aid instead of stressing the need for maximum mobilization of Latin-American productive potential, for combating the squandering of resources, for restricting the conspicuous consumption of the wealthy, and for putting a stop to the siphoning off of savings through unfavorable foreign trade and even more harmful international capital movements.

Pan-Americanism ignored the subject of democracy for a long time. The first isolated references to it were made in the meetings at Buenos Aires (1936), Havana (1940), and Mexico City (1945). It was in the Rio Treaty of 1947, however, that for the first time, it was declared that "the obligation of mutual assistance and common defense of the American republics is essentially related to their democratic ideals." And Article 5 of the Bogotá Charter went even further, establishing that "the solidarity of the American States and the exalted ends pursued thereby require the political organization of these states on a basis of effective exercise of democracy."

Most important—and, at the same time, most dangerous—was Resolution XXXII on the "Preservation and Defense of

Democracy in America," adopted at Bogotá. In essence, it was agreed:

1. To condemn the methods of any system which tends to suppress political and civil rights and liberties, particularly the activities of international Communism.

2. To adopt the necessary measures to eradicate and prevent activities directed, aided, or instigated by foreign governments, organizations, or individuals which tend to subvert institutions, to foment discord in internal political life, or to disturb through pressure, subversive propaganda, threats, or any other means, the right of peoples to govern themselves in accordance with democratic aspirations.

The introductory section of the resolution stressed that: "The present world situation calls for . . . urgent measures to proscribe the tactics of totalitarian hegemony . . . and to prevent the agents of international Communism or of any other totalitarianism from trying to undermine the free and authentic will of the peoples of this continent.

"Because of its anti-democratic nature and interventionistic tendency, the political action of international Communism or of any totalitarianism is incompatible with the concept of American freedom."

The Bogotá meeting was the first in which "international Communism" was openly condemned and also the first in which such condemnation was linked to the defense of democracy. Thus, the Churchill and Truman Doctrines were shifted to the inter-American plane. And these were not to remain mere unilateral declarations of intention but to be converted into actual international agreements, based upon a common strategy against a supposed common enemy. This called for mechanically carrying over two fundamental and basically exclusive concepts: The Anglo-Saxon versions of "Communism" and "democracy."

The Bogotá agreement was not received with unanimous enthusiasm, however. It was accepted out of weakness, fear, and defeatism, because the United States offered financial aid in exchange for political solidarity. But the danger was recognized in many circles and it was realized that a great deal had been handed over for very little. Doubts were expressed as to whether democracy was being defended.

Luis Quintanilla, for example, wrote: "The problem is complex. Where is the country . . . that can sincerely present itself as a model of democracy? . . . Could anybody, now or in the future, conceive an unchangeable model for democracy which would exclude any possibility of peaceful, or even revolutionary, popular changes? . . . Is it advisable for America to assume the responsibility of fixing a uniform type of government for the American states? . . . We are inclined to say no."[5]

The design of arbitrarily imposing the classical Anglo-Saxon pattern of democracy on America was also criticized in the United States. Sumner Welles wrote at the time: "What guarantee do we have that permits us to suppose that a form of democracy that has evolved gradually to meet the needs of the English-speaking nations should for that reason answer in identical fashion the needs of peoples with absolutely different origins, traditions, and cultures? If we seek now to restrict the right of the peoples of Latin America to support or overthrow their own governments we will be destroying the regional system of the New World."[6]

The fight against Communism admitted the use of any kind of weapon, and when the resolution referred to was approved, it was remarked that the reality of the danger had been witnessed by the delegates to the ninth conference who saw innocent blood flowing in the streets of Bogotá because of a "Communist" coup. As a matter of fact, the capital of Colombia went through days of unrest and anxiety because of the assassination of the popular and respected liberal leader, Jorge Eliécer Gaitán, and the understandable reaction of protest this provoked among the people. The so-called *bogotazo* [*azo*, a slang suffix meaning "a blow"] was not plotted by international Communism, or even by the Left of Colombia, but by terrorists linked to the traditional conservative groups. The incident was useful: public order had been disrupted. What mattered least was the real source of the disturbances; the important thing was to blame them on international Communism thus enabling the United States to carry out its foreign policy and convince Latin America that what Marshall had said in Bogotá about "the deliberate and open opposition of the Soviet Union to world recovery and peace" was true.

The Chapultepec, Rio, and Bogotá conferences gave the Monroeist concept of Pan-Americanism a great boost; they contributed to the establishment of a new system of military cooperation and made it possible for the United States to obtain more than it had in years past, although some Latin Americans considered it worthwhile to pay such a price in exchange for indispensable technical and financial cooperation.

The year after the Bogotá conference, President Truman announced a program of technical assistance, known thereafter as Point Four, which supported the idea prevalent among certain circles that new prospects of cooperation and development were opening. He said solemnly, before the Congress of his country: "We must embark on a bold new program for making the benefits of our scientific advances and industrial progress available for the improvement and growth of underdeveloped areas . . . we should foster capital investment in areas needing development. . . . The old imperialism—exploitation for foreign profits—has no place in our plans."[7]

Would the United States return to the democratic course initiated by Roosevelt and to the policy of unity in the struggle against Fascism? Would a policy truly capable of overcoming the backwardness of colonial and semicolonial countries be initiated? These conjectures were short-lived. United States officials, as well as businessmen, were explicit and soon let it be seen that the plan was neither new nor bold. The aim was to confront underdevelopment with a single weapon: Stimula-

tion of United States private investments abroad in order that
its "know-how" and "spirit of progress" should be the main
lever in developing Latin America, Asia, and Africa. The old
imperialism was not dead; it had only been replaced by a new
imperialism. Point Four was just another instrument of
United States foreign policy and its anti-Communist strategy.

This was so far removed from being the point of departure
of anything new and encouraging which could effectively contribute to progress and the preservation of peace that, a few
weeks later, even as peace advocates were appealing to the
great powers for unity and understanding, the North Atlantic
Pact (NATO) was signed in Washington.

Unquestionably a further step toward the preparation of a
third war, this pact was presented as a "contribution to the
cause of peace" and "an act of faith in the destiny of Western
civilization." Actually, it was a revealing indication of lack of
faith in civilization, of fear of social progress, and of the determination of the United States to revive the Cold War and
deepen the controversy within the United Nations.

As was inevitable once Fascism had been defeated, popular
and revolutionary forces made significant advances between
1946 and 1949. Nationalist groups in India were notably
strengthened; land reform was instituted by the Guatemalan
revolution; the forces which had fought most effectively
against Nazism took power in one Eastern European country
after another and launched ambitious development plans; a
movement bringing new life to Korea triumphed; and the
revolution in China won a tremendous popular victory.

In accordance with United States strategy after 1945, all
of these advances, far from being considered progress and a
step forward in the struggle for peace, were looked on as new
threats to the interests of the United States and the major
industrial countries of the West in general. Actually it was
this attitude that prompted the creation of the Atlantic Pact,
patterned after the Rio de Janeiro Treaty even to its system
of operation; it also incorporated the principle by which an

"armed attack" against any of the signatory nations would be considered an attack on all and would call for measures which included the use of military force.

The Atlantic Pact was a new step backward. Presented hypocritically as a simple defense agreement, it was in fact another device for furthering the fight against socialism and the national liberation movements, and it was a real threat to the internal freedom of every country and to the principle of nonintervention. It crystallized the "fraternal association" Churchill had proposed in Fulton, Missouri, three years before, and the division of the United Nations into two factions. From the moment the pact was signed, all ideas of dealing with the economic recession, which was sharpening at the time, through constructive measures which would not require rearmament as a means of achieving high living standards and high income and employment levels for the people of the United States were abandoned.

The consequences of the United States belligerent policy soon made their appearance in Latin America. In April 1951, in the midst of the Korean War, the Fourth Meeting of Foreign Ministers was held in Washington to discuss the necessity for "swift action" against the "aggressive activities of international communism" which, according to the American ministers, "disturb the peace . . . and threaten freedom and democracy."

It has been seen how Latin America's subordination to the anti-Communist strategy of the United States became more marked in the meetings between 1945 and 1948. Nevertheless, the resolutions taken in Washington were far graver than any that had come before. The central thesis of the assembly was the grave threat posed by Communism to the peace of the continent and the urgent need to take defensive measures. No one really discussed whether such a thesis had any validity or not. Some delegates probably had doubts but did not dare express them. As before, in Rio and Bogotá, the Latin-American representatives asked United States imperialism for financial aid in exchange for political solidarity.

What measures were adopted in Washington? Among the most important were the following:

1. To assign to the Inter-American Joint Defense Board the "military planning of the common defense."

2. To recommend to all governments that they maintain adequate representation on the Board, actively support its work, and cooperate with it in order to establish "a coordinated system for the exchange of appropriate information."

3. To recommend to the governments themselves that they examine their laws and regulations and adopt "those changes . . . necessary for insuring that the subversive activities . . . of international Communism . . . can be . . . prevented and sanctioned; and that measures be taken to regulate . . . the transit . . . of foreigners who can be reasonably suspected of attempting subversive acts." [8]

As Narciso Bassols remarked, "The time had come in the program for the preparation of the Third World War—as far as this continent is concerned—to move on from words to deeds; it was indispensable to establish the political and technical foundations for the regimentation of the economies of the Latin-American countries, suppliers of raw materials and buyers of manufactured goods, in order to guarantee their efficiency as purveyors of metals and agricultural products while at the same time setting forth the political and military terms of Latin-American collaboration in belligerent undertakings."[9]

In fact, in addition to reaffirming the Monroe Doctrine at the Washington meeting, President Truman said: "In these uneasy times, production for defense depends on our economic strength. We need to increase production of strategic raw materials . . . we must establish the principle of the equitable sharing of this responsibility."[10]

The Fourth Meeting of Foreign Ministers accomplished its purpose of incorporating Latin America directly into a policy against its own interests, abetted by the impotent and cowardly silence of the Latin-American delegates who, as in so many other instances, seemed incapable of standing up and speaking out with dignity. But even in those difficult moments, honest Latin-American voices like those of Bassols and others were raised despite the curtain of silence and the smokescreen of lies and half-truths.

The distinguished Guatemalan writer, Luis Cardoza y Aragón, for instance, said, "There were three topics on the agenda of the Conference of Foreign Ministers . . . and the United States Department of State obtained the unanimous surrender of Latin America in all three. For this reason, the democratic forces consider this Conference a most serious setback for Latin-American diplomacy and politics.

"Democracy has been destroyed . . . in almost all our countries. Point Two of the Conference of Foreign Ministers will serve to persecute the forces representing democracy under the pretext of the Communist spectre, the danger of war, and any kind of humbug they wish."[11]

And Jesús Silva Herzog wrote: "The truth did not shine at the Conference of Foreign Ministers. It seems doubtful that the Latin-American people will be able to wave . . . the flag of victory as a result of this meeting. What is certain is that we shall sell raw materials in exchange for finished products . . . that we shall have large, brand-new and well-equipped armies which will not infrequently serve to oppress the people more, to consolidate the tyrants in power, and to send the Indian of Guatemala, Peru, and other countries to fight and die in distant lands in defense of 'the American way of life,' for the sake of benefits he never enjoyed."[12]

Another illustrious Mexican, Luis Cabrera, also spoke out during the days of the Conference: "In Washington . . . there will be no discussion . . . as to whether a continental danger really exists; if the next war is inevitable; if the moment has come to go to the aid of a neighbor. . . . War has already been decided on by the United States and it has been determined that the Latin-American vassals shall make their contributions of armed men to their feudal lord. The United States thinks like the Marquis de Croix, a famous viceroy of New Spain, who said, 'Once and for all, let the Hispanic-American vassals know that they were born to hold their tongues and obey, and not to argue or offer opinions.' "

To which Cabrera added optimistically and with conviction: "The 'manifest destiny' defeatists believe that the United States will crush any move made by Mexico to become independent of her; not by force of arms, any more, but with the economic might of the dollar. I believe, on the contrary, that Latin America can win its independence. And further, I believe that . . . this is the propitious moment to give the shout of independence. What happens is that we are cowards and do not know our own strength."[13]

It was clearly demonstrated at the Meeting of Foreign Ministers in 1951 that technical and financial aid from the United States was not only subject to reimbursement but contingent upon political and military cooperation. Despite its gravity, United States intervention in Korea was still something remote and vague to Latin Americans. The obligations they had assumed seemed at times to be mere formalities; and subordination to anti-Communist strategy something related to what was going on in the Orient rather than on American soil. As for the war, though long and bloody, it was not only taking place thousands of miles away, but it was improving prices and terms of trade. But hardly had the conflict ended in Korea than the principal target of United States interest was again located on the American continent—after the tenth Pan-American Conference in Caracas in 1954. This target was Guatemala.

During the long and bloody dictatorships in the Guatemala of Jorge Ubico (1931–1944) and Manuel Estrada Cabrera (1898–1920) before him, the United States had never found cause for complaint, nor did it ever consider that any threat to freedom and democracy existed in those or any other tyrannical governments.

The victory of the 1944 revolution was at first regarded in official United States circles as the exercise by the Guatemalan people of their right of self-determination, despite the fact that there was no lack of insidious voices to envelop the events in hostility and often distort what was happening. However, this attitude changed as the revolution gained headway; the greater the undermining of Roosevelt's policy, the greater the hostility of the State Department. Each new progressive measure adopted in Guatemala aroused the same response in the reactionary groups revolving around the United Fruit Company and the United States Embassy—Communism! If the government launched a literacy campaign, the response was not long in coming—Communism! When land reform was announced —Communism! When all political parties were to be guaranteed the right to support and disseminate their platforms— Communism! Everything was Communism, including organization of the peasants and guaranteeing the workers their most basic rights. But the revolution continued its course, fulfilling its objectives.

At the end of his term, President Juan José Arévalo (1944– 1945) declared:

> I had the conviction then, and I still have, that a nation cannot be free until all its inhabitants are made free, one by one. To achieve this in Guatemala we had to clash with the particular social and economic structure of the country whose culture, politics, and economy were in the hands of three hundred families. . . .
> I could not tell you if what we achieved in Guatemala should be labeled democracy or something resembling that. Professors of political theory will find a name for it. But if through the ineffable workings of conceptual habit or for the sake of linguistic convenience, it should be named "democracy," I call upon you for multitudinous testimony to the effect that this Guatemalan democracy was not Hitlerian nor Carthaginian.[14]

Cardoza y Aragón, commenting on the Arévalo administration, wrote in 1956: "Guatemala managed to defend itself for nine and a half years against the constantly coordinated internal and external conspiracy. No democracy was ever persecuted

with the anathema visited upon the Guatemalan government.
. . . It was saved on many occasions . . . despite the fifth
column infiltrating it from top to bottom." He also recalled
that in 1953, after a scandalous newspaper campaign, Spruille
Braden, public relations chief of the United Fruit Company,
called for United States intervention in Latin America, and
particularly in Guatemala.[15]

What happened in Washington, Bogotá, and Rio de Janeiro
was more or less repeated in Caracas in 1954. Latin America
was expecting a program of international economic cooperation to come out of the conference, but once more the United
States placed its interests above those of the continent and
turned the meeting into another battleground against the
alleged penetration of international Communism.

The attitude the United States would take at the conference
was clearly manifested even before it began. In January, 1954,
the Ambassador to Guatemala declared cynically: "Public
opinion in the United States might force us to take some
measures to prevent Guatemala from falling into the lap of
international Communism."[16] And when the meeting opened,
John Foster Dulles said, "There is not a single country in
this hemisphere which has not been penetrated by the apparatus of international Communism, acting under orders from
Moscow."[17] It would have been difficult to be more explicit:
"Communist aggression" was in sight and it was obvious that
it had to be met. Despite Dulles' melodramatic vehemence
and the pressure exercised by the United States to win fol-
lowers, unconditional support was forthcoming only from the
"representative democracies" of Nicaragua, Santo Domingo,
El Salvador, Colombia, Cuba, Peru, and Venezuela. At that
time, Venezuela was under the popularly repudiated regime
of Marcos Pérez Jiménez who had nevertheless been named
Honorary President of the American [United States] Club of
Caracas a few months prior to the conference; in honor of the

occasion, Ambassador Fletcher Warren paid him special homage for "his services to the cause of democracy,"[18] and *Time* and other United States publications awarded him a medal for "civic merit."

The main political resolution of the tenth Pan-American Conference was the so-called Declaration of Caracas which brought anti-Communist strategy up to date. In the draft presented by the United States, which was finally approved with merely formalistic amendments, it was provided:

> That the domination or control of the political institutions of any American State by the international communist movement, extending to this hemisphere the political system of an extra-continental power, would constitute a threat to sovereignty and political independence . . . endangering the peace of America, and would call for a meeting of consultation to consider the adoption of appropriate action in accordance with existing treaties.

Argentina, Mexico, and, of course, Guatemala, recognized what was entailed in the Dulles proposal and criticized it accordingly. Mexico, in particular, proposed some amendments aimed at securing greater precision in the wording of the text and at establishing the point that measures adopted against Communism in each country should be in accord with their national legislation. Although Mexico placed its anti-Communist position on record when one of its most prominent delegates declared that: "We are all aware and absolutely convinced about having to unite our efforts to repel it. . . . America must be united against the Communist danger," Foster Dulles termed the Mexican amendments "vague, legalistic, incredible, and unacceptable."[19]

The Mexican delegation declared:

> Mexico will not support the proposal of the United States with its affirmative vote because the form in which it is worded could give rise to interventions in any of our countries, such as no American state should suffer. . . . We are afraid that future interpretation of this document might contain elements that could provoke intervention against a government which is

accused of being Communist merely because it tries, fully
within its rights, to win its economic independence and to
combat capitalist interests within its own territory. This is not
purely hyopthetical; we have seen it happen in the past. Mexico
has suffered interventions in its territory and these have been
extra-continental and by countries of this hemisphere. We know
what we are talking about; we know that if we want American
unity it is impossible to leave the door open so that intervention may be resorted to again at any given moment.[20]

The Guatemalan position was even more sharply defined.
As soon as he arrived in Caracas, Foreign Minister Guillermo
Toriello declared:

> The Guatemalan delegation will categorically oppose any
> resolution or declaration which, on the pretext of Communism,
> may contravene the fundamental principles of democracy, pos-
> tulate violation of the rights of man, or infringe the principle
> of nonintervention, and which tends to convert Pan Amer-
> icanism into an instrument for maintaining the peoples of Latin
> America in semicolonial conditions for the benefit of the power-
> ful interests of foreign monopolies. We oppose . . . emphatically
> the internationalization of McCarthyism, the burning of books,
> and the imposition of stereotyped thinking. And we denounce
> before this conference and before the conscience of America, the
> political aggression and threats of economic aggression and
> intervention of which the Republic of Guatemala is the victim.[21]

Guatemala argued irrefutably that the Declaration of
Caracas was not a resolution against international Communism but was actually against the Guatemalan Revolution,
against the principles of self-determination and nonintervention and against the foundations upon which true democracy
rests. The Caracas agreements not only implied the Pan-Americanization of Monroeism, but as the Guatemalan delegation
put it, the "internationalization of McCarthyism." Particularly
the resolution against Communism, perhaps the most anti-
democratic measure adopted up to then in the history of Pan-
Americanism sought, as Toriello pointed out, "to restrict all
the fundamental freedoms of man, recognized and guaranteed
by all nations," and to add a reservation to each to the effect

that "freedom of thought exists, but not for Communists; freedom of movement exists, but not for Communists; freedom of association is guaranteed, but not for Communists; all citizens may exercise their political rights except Communists."[22]

The principle of nonintervention which had for the first time in Bogotá been recognized as a fundamental principle of international law on the American continent crumbled in Caracas. The anti-Communist declaration represented a danger to the exercise of fundamental democratic freedoms and constituted an unacceptable form of intervention which violated sovereignty under the pretext of combating Communist propaganda. In reference to this declaration, Isidro Fabela wrote soon after the conference: "Is this not McCarthyism extended to the entire Latin continent? . . . Is this not intervention in the internal affairs of independent states? Obviously it is."[23]

And, recalling the dangerous implications of the declaration—in view of the mechanisms of the Rio Treaty—even for other countries which, like Mexico and Argentina, had abstained from voting, Fabela also declared: "The most decisive way of avoiding the danger of violations of our basic law . . . would be to *denounce the Rio de Janeiro Treaty . . . which would free Mexico of a very heavy burden,* since such a denunciation would be the only way of defending nonintervention in view of the fact that the Caracas resolution, *ipso facto,* gives the Rio Treaty disproportionate scope . . . and completely perverts its intention."[24]

Some months after the United States triumph in Caracas, the United Fruit Company was to score its success in Guatemala, after a battle which former President Arévalo described as follows:

The date set for the invasion of Guatemala was public knowledge. The arms which were to support the army of "liberation" were rushed to Honduras and Nicaragua. Three days before the invasion, Herr Goebbels (I mean Foster Dulles) declared that

Guatemala had fallen under a kind of terrorist government, since anti-Communists were fleeing the country. . . .

On June 18, forty-eight hours after General Eisenhower's signal, Yankee planes manned by United States pilots began bombing—the first bombardment of Central America. "Operation Guatemala" had begun.[25]

Colonel Castillo Armas was to consummate the coup against the government of President Arbenz and, a few days later, win what Foster Dulles, connected with United Fruit for many years, was to call a "glorious victory." The assault had been perpetrated: Guatemala was liberated from Communism, as foreseen in Caracas, and restored to its former freedom of living in subjugation to the United Fruit Company, the old reactionary oligarchy, and the State Department. Castillo Armas' death some months later was considered by Eisenhower "a great loss to his own nation and to the entire Free World."[26] He was a man who had come to power with no standing or popular support. Monroeist Pan-Americanism once more prevailed over Bolivarism and the democratic American tradition. Against the background of the resentment, discontent, and heightened awareness of the peoples of Latin America, a phrase of Bolívar's in a letter he wrote to Sir Patrick Campbell in 1829 stood out vividly in its unaltered timeliness: "The United States seems destined by Providence to plague America with misery in the name of liberty."

Notes

[1] "Bases Constitucionales de la OEA," by Pablo Campos Ortiz, in *México en la IX Conferencia Internacional Americana*, Mexico, 1948, p. 40.

[2] *Ibid.*, p. 51.

[3] "El Convenio Económico de Bogotá," by Gilberto Loyo, in *México en la IX Conferencia Internacional Americana*, pp. 205–208.

[4] "El Problema de las Inversiones Extranjeras," by Antonio Carrillo Flores, in *México en la IX Conferencia . . .* , p. 228.

[5] Luis Quintanilla, *op. cit.*, pp. 63, 78.

[6] *The Washington Post*, December 28, 1948.

[7] *Readings in American Foreign Policy*, p. 541–543.

[8] Official Documents of the Fourth Meeting.

[9] *Obras*, p. 920.

10 "La Reunión de Cancilleres," *Cuadernos Americanos*, Mexico, May-June, 1951, p. 58.
11 "La Conferencia de Cancilleres: su significación para América Latina," by Luis Cardoza y Aragón, in *Cuadernos Americanos*, Mexico, May–June, 1951, pp. 70–71, 78–79.
12 "Mi Cuarto a Espadas," by Jesús Silva Herzog in *Cuadernos Americanos*, May–June, 1951, p. 83.
13 *Una opinión mexicana sobre el conflicto mundial*, by Luis Cabrera (Blas Urrea), Mexico, 1951, pp. 79–81.
14 *La Revolución Guatemalteca*, by Luis Cardoza y Aragón, Montevideo, 1956, pp. 85–86.
15 *Ibid.*, pp. 89–97.
16 J. Gerassi, *op. cit.*, p. 219.
17 L. Mecham, *op. cit.*, p. 441.
18 O. Waiss. *op. cit.*, p. 109.
19 *La Conferencia de Caracas y la actitud anticomunista de México*, by Isidro Fabela, Mexico, 1954, p. 15.
20 *México en la Conferencia Interamericana*, Ministry of Foreign Relations, Mexico, 1958.
21 *La Batalla de Guatemala*, by Guillermo Toriello, Mexico, 1955, p. 94.
22 *Ibid.*, p. 127.
23 *La Conferencia de Caracas*, by Isidro Fabela, p. 18.
24 *Ibid.*
25 *Guatemala, la Democracia y el Imperio*, by Juan José Arévalo, Mexico, 1954, pp. 135–136.
26 J. Gerassi, *op. cit.*, p. 223.

9. Reform or Revolution?

United States pressure, as well as demands for economic aid from Latin-American governments, increased after the Caracas conference. The years of World War II and even those immediately following had been relatively prosperous for Latin America. Although it was true that profound economic imbalances were produced and social inequality sharpened during that period, economic development was relatively rapid and between 1942 and 1951 annual national income reached a growth rate of over 6 percent.

Toward 1947, however, the effects of a severe inflation which had been in the making since 1939 became more acute and, despite stabilizing measures, there were currency devaluations in Mexico, Colombia, Argentina, Chile, and other countries between 1948 and 1950. During those years, the rate of investment in Latin America dropped appreciably, coinciding with the economic recession in the United States which ended with the initiation of the Korean War.

From 1952 on, and especially after 1956–57, the situation became even more unfavorable. The drop in price of sugar, meat, wool, and other products was followed by a slump in cotton, lead, tin, and finally, by a generalized decline which seriously affected terms of trade; the price index sagged from 109 to 92, representing an average yearly loss to Latin America of $1.5 billion.[1]

Between 1957 and 1961 alone, Latin-American gold and dollar reserves decreased by approximately $1 billion; the per capita growth rate of the national product, which had been 3.5 percent between 1940 and 1950, dropped to 2.2 percent during 1951–55, to 1.4 percent in 1956–57, and to less than

1 percent between 1958 and 1961.[2] Simultaneously, both agricultural and industrial production lagged in the majority of
the countries, and inflation caused dislocations which in turn
produced growing popular discontent and increasing political
tension, often expressed through the adoption of repressive,
frankly anti-democratic measures against the vain attempts of
the workers to defend the purchasing power of their wages and
their share in national income.

The ephemeral boom accompanying the Korean War was
hardly over when Latin-American governments began making
certain demands. At the meetings of the Inter-American
Economic and Social Council held in Panama, Caracas, and
Rio de Janeiro in 1952, 1953, and 1954, respectively, Latin
America demanded better prices for its raw materials, economic and financial aid, technical assistance within the UN
program and Point Four and, in addition, a mechanism which
would sustain the purchasing power of its declining monetary
reserves. But, as was so often the case, the final agreements
reached at these meetings were unsatisfactory and everything
was left in the form of studies, promises, recommendations,
good wishes, and noncommittal declarations.

The sharpening of economic and financial difficulties in the
Latin-American countries after 1956, together with the inde-
cisiveness and ineptitude of the governing groups in getting
to the bottom of the most serious problems, contributed to
the accentuation of the various forms of Latin-American
dependence. There was apparent everywhere a growing interest in obtaining money from the United States as the only
way to get out of the crisis and to achieve appreciable economic development within a short period. The same tune was
repeated over and over again: Latin America lacked savings
and capital and only investments and loans from abroad could
fill the gap. Under such conditions, to argue the truth of this
or to discuss other measures was secondary and irrelevant. It
was no time for speculation or even for reflection. All that
counted was action, the exertion of pressure, and the acquisi-

tion of foreign economic aid as rapidly as possible, in exchange, of course, for political collaboration—collaboration which, as Torres Bodet had stated in Rio a few years before, was 50 percent of American solidarity.

Under the Kubitschek government in Brazil, a more urgent and ambitious plan began to take shape to obtain larger investments and loans from the United States. It was named "Operation Pan-America," as though to point up the great urgency and strategic character of the plan.

"Operation Pan-America" did not succeed in arousing much interest, nor did it change the existing situation. It was mentioned at various OAS meetings and often given flashy propaganda, but it received only bureaucratic attention in the United States because, in the end, the United States maintained its traditional position—that of insisting that the best means of speeding up development and of tackling financial problems and balance of payments maladjustment was to attract private foreign investments.

Latin America kept insisting on economic aid, while the United States demanded political collaboration in defense of its international position under Foster Dulles' slogan, "We do not have friends, we have interests"; in adopting new measures to defend the "security of the continent"; and in drawing the politically influential Latin-American officer corps closer to the United States, in the hope that they would exclude Soviet influence, give the United States their support, maintain political stability, ensure continued access to strategic raw materials and provide rights to the use of bases.[3]

In August-September 1957, a new inter-American economic meeting was held in Buenos Aires at which the draft of an agreement and a declaration were worked out. Once more, discussion revolved around the advantages of creating an inter-American bank, of increasing trade, easing restrictions, and facilitating exchange of raw materials, capital, and techniques. But again political pressure reared its head, showing up this time in an apparently innocuous proposal by President

Prado of Peru to link OAS and NATO. It was immediately approved by the United States, but the majority of the Latin-American countries opposed it. Mexico, for example, argued that whereas an exchange of information was acceptable, the same did not apply to "the establishment of political, economic, and military ties between the OAS and NATO," because while the former was a permanent organization created with certain objectives, NATO was a "temporary body for armed defense."[4]

In September 1958, the Foreign Ministers of the continent met in Washington to give formal approval to "Operation Pan-America" and agreed to a meeting of the so-called Committee of 21 in December of the same year. Again, certain hopes were raised at the meeting, but these were not long in evaporating. At the closing session, the President of Colombia, Alfonso López, declared: "Perhaps it is better that we go home. . . . I had hopes, great expectations. I was mistaken."[5] And while Latin-American governments tried in vain to obtain economic and financial cooperation, Eisenhower was writing Juscelino Kubitschek asking him for "a reaffirmation of devotion to Pan-Americanism."[6]

However, it was not a propitious time to make such a reaffirmation. While bargaining was going on between the United States and the governments of Latin America, an adventure story became reality in Cuba, culminating in a victorious revolution which was to give rise to an entirely new situation in America. In 1953, a group of young men led by Fidel Castro, ready to give their lives for their country's freedom, made an heroic assault on the Moncada army barracks. The exploit was suicidal, but several of the attackers survived. Castro was jailed and in delivering his own defense plea, without doubt one of the great messages of Latin America, he said:

> How can anything justify Batista in power which he took against the will of the people and by violating the laws of the republic through treachery and force? How can a bloody, op-

pressive, and ignorant regime be considered legitimate? How can a government be called revolutionary which is compounded of the most backward methods, ideas, and men in public life? How can the high treason of a court whose mission was to defend our Constitution be considered legally valid? By what right does it jail citizens who were ready to give their blood and their lives for the decency of their country? This is monstrous in the eyes of the nation and in the light of the principles of true justice!

And he ended by saying, "Condemn me! It does not matter! History will absolve me!"[7]

After nearly two years in jail, Castro was released and from that moment he started to prepare the revolution against the Batista dictatorship. He went to New York to obtain help from the Cuban residents there and later traveled to Mexico, where he organized the expedition of the "Granma" which ended in the Sierra Maestra on Christmas, 1956. In 1958, the government was still trying to mislead public opinion by alleging that the rebels had been completely routed; after January 2, 1959, the victorious rebel army poured into the streets of Havana in one of the most spontaneous and extraordinary popular manifestations ever recorded in the history of people's struggles for independence.

The Cuban Revolution was received with enthusiasm throughout Latin America and with understandable reserve, but not yet outright hostility, in the United States. As he had announced he would at the Moncada trial in 1953, Castro started to change things rapidly. His actions were aimed at restoring and enforcing the 1940 Constitution and especially at cleaning up the administration of justice, initiating land reform, granting the workers and employees of the large enterprises a share in the profits, improving the conditions of the sugar producers, confiscating the ill-gotten properties and fortunes of public officials and businessmen, and establishing an international policy of friendship and solidarity with all the countries of the continent.

As Castro said in 1959: "The Cuban people want something more than a mere change of command. Cuba is anxious for a radical change in all fields. . . . The people must be given something more than freedom and democracy in the abstract; they must be provided with a decent way of life."[8]

A few months later, he was to explain: "As soon as we started to make revolutionary laws, they began accusing us of being Communists. . . . And what is behind this accusation? The same thing as is behind what reaction has done all over the world. . . . When it finds itself impotent to defend its privileges inside the country, it appeals outside."[9]

As the Cuban Revolution advanced in one of the fastest and most spectacular processes in modern history, United States imperialism started attacking it with all the means at its disposal. Toward the middle of 1959, the fifth Consultative Meeting of Foreign Ministers was held in Santiago, Chile, where a resolution was adopted on "Guaranteeing Peace and Perfecting American Solidarity," and the need was reiterated for defining and preserving "representative democracy" and preventing Cuba from taking an "inconvenient" path. The weakness of the Foreign Ministers was evident; their efforts toward obtaining United States investments and credits had made headway—consequently they were obliged to cast aside all dignity and acknowledge Cuba's new *independent* path as ill-advised.

The defense of "representative democracy" did not end with the Santiago agreements. It assumed new forms from that point on: Campaigns of slander; aid and protection for the war criminals and saboteurs who went on bombing expeditions from Florida; breaking off of ordinary business credits; violation of territorial waters; and repeated threats of intervention.[10]

In August, 1960, San José, Costa Rica was the stage for the first great inter-American battle against Cuba; the Santiago meeting had been merely a feint. Venezuela accused the Trujillo dictatorship in Santo Domingo of intervening in her internal affairs in violation of the provisions of the UN and

OAS charters. The accusation was justified and, although up until a few months before the United States had defended Trujillo and hailed him as one of its main allies in the fight against Communism, at the sixth Consultative Meeting in San José it approved sanctions against Santo Domingo in order to prepare the way for its own attack on Cuba; this was, unquestionably, what brought the ministers to Costa Rica.

The moment land reform was initiated, United States interests, which had controlled a large part of the sugar plantations and the sugar industry of Cuba for over half a century were, of course, threatened, and United States policy toward the new government became increasingly hostile.

At the seventh Consultative Meeting held in San José on the following day, the delegation from Cuba attended in order to denounce, courageously and resolutely, the aggressive policy of United States imperialism.

The Cuban Foreign Minister, Raúl Roa, said at the meeting:

> The revolutionary government of Cuba has not come to San José de Costa Rica as the defendant but as the prosecutor. It is here in order to speak out its relentless *j'accuse* against the richest, most powerful, and most aggressive capitalist power in the world; a power which has failed to intimidate, to force to its knees, or to buy off the revolutionary government. . . .
>
> The cunning weapon wielded by United States propaganda against the Cuban Revolution . . . has been . . . to brand it indiscriminately as "influenced by Communists," as acting as a "Soviet satellite" or "the spearhead of international Communism." This is the scratched record we have been listening to in crescendo for seventeen months. . . .
>
> In the name of the revolutionary government of Cuba, I accuse the government of the United States of making this false charge in order to first safeguard and then recuperate the privileges of exploiting corporations who carry more weight with the State Department than the legitimate interests of the people of the United States. . . . The revolution brought by the people shoulder to shoulder with Fidel Castro is as Cuban as the Sierra Maestra, as American as the Andes, and as universal as the lofty human values it embodies.[11]

The seventh Consultative Meeting of Foreign Ministers took place in a tense atmosphere, charged with passion and prejudice. The charges brought by Cuba did not seem to the ministers to merit their attention, much less their careful study, and from the very outset it became evident that the defendant on trial was Cuba, which had come to the conference as the prosecutor.

The government of the United States was not only unwilling to accept or even permit investigation of any of the charges, but was determined to act as prosecutor in the name of a new "threat to the peace and security of the continent." The position of George Christian Herter, then Secretary of State, left no room for doubts. One of his theses was: "The installation of a Communist regime in any American republic could automatically involve the loss of that country's independence in foreign relations and to a large degree in its domestic affairs."[12] And in two draft resolutions, one dealing with "the adherence of member states to the principles of representative democracy" and the other with the question of "the Sino-Soviet bloc's interference in inter-American affairs," the United States managed to set up the point which dominated the debates of the conference. The second of these draft proposals urged Cuba to "revoke all alliances with the said extra-continental powers and show that it would return to faithful adherence to inter-American principles." Castro's "contempt" for the OAS, illustrated in his declaration that "Cuba would continue to be a friend of the USSR and of China because these countries were Cuba's friends," was censured along with his "political and economic subversion," and it was established that relations with such countries were not acts of sovereignty but "interference," and "a direct breach of the basic principle of the inter-American system and a threat to the peace and security of the American states."[13]

After lengthy discussions in which the subordination of Latin-American governments to the United States was again evident, the Declaration of San José was adopted. Among

other things, it decreed that "acceptance of a threat of extra-
continental intervention . . . endangers American security and
. . . obliges the OAS to firmly disapprove and reject it"; that
the inter-American system is "incompatible with all forms of
totalitarianism"; and that "it is the obligation of the member
states to submit to the discipline of the system."

The Declaration did not mention Cuba, but there was no
doubt what it referred to. The Cuban delegation protested
sharply and walked out of the conference. Raúl Roa said:

> What they claim to be defending here are not democratic
> American institutions but imperialist interests and the so-called
> American way of life. . . . This implies the conviction that
> United States democratic institutions in their present form have
> attained the maximum possible development and are susceptible
> of no transformation, thereby creating, in order to preserve
> them, a system . . . similar to the Holy Alliance. . . . This
> miserable farce of a new Holy Alliance of semicolonial countries
> in defense of the political institutions of their metropolis during
> the very days when the majority of the Latin-American nations
> are celebrating the sesquicentennial anniversary of their struggle
> for independence, is really pitiful.[14]

The San José Conference was a typical inter-American
meeting. Imperialism again had its way and, as so often before,
operated behind a screen of soft-spoken and hypocritical
verbiage, using a cat's-paw to get its chestnuts out of the fire.
Evaluating results at the close of the meeting, the Ecuadorian
delegate said: "There are reasons for being truly regretful. I
refer to the absence of Cuba which left its seat empty at this
conference . . . at which there neither were nor could be
accusers or accused."[15] And in the course of the meeting, when
it was easy to guess what type of agreements were going to be
reached, *Time* magazine, ironically making it appear that the
resolutions against Cuba and the principles of self-determination were the product not of the Monroe version of Pan-
Americanism but of the American libertarian tradition, wrote:
"The inter-American system that has produced the OAS was
invented by South America's George Washington, Simón Bolí-

var."[16] A vain attempt to transform Bolívar into the Father of the OAS! As vain as that of those who, incapable of understanding the deep roots and irrepressible surge of the Cuban Revolution, sought at the time demogogically to counterpose Martí's ideology against that which was at last crystallizing, that for which the Apostle had given his life.

The San José meeting was another victory for aggressive Pan-Americanism. It highlighted the fact that the United States had no intention of yielding an inch; that the war against Cuba was to the death; and that maintaining the *status quo* in Latin America (the privileges and the vested interests) under the deceitful slogans of "representative democracy" and "hemispheric solidarity" was far more important than the principle of national sovereignty which only Cuba defended openly. The disagreements heard in Caracas were no longer raised in San José. In Caracas, Mexico and Argentina still stood with Guatemala on fundamental issues. In San José, Cuba was alone with no one really on its side (although Foreign Ministers Arcaya of Venezuela and Roa of Peru refused to sign the Final Act) except for the peoples of America who understood that it was not just the Cuban Revolution that was on the stand, but all of Latin America as well as the principle of self-determination and the right of peoples to choose the government and the economic and social system they wish.

On March 13, 1961, the President of the United States, John F. Kennedy, addressed the people of the hemisphere, calling on them to "join in a new alliance for progress, in a vast cooperative effort without parallel in its magnitude and lofty purpose." And he added, his voice charged with emotion, "Let us reawaken our American Revolution, that it may guide the people's struggle everywhere, not by an imperialism of force or by fear, but by courage, freedom, and hope in man's future." Kennedy's words could not but encourage certain hopes and lead people to think for a moment that the United States would abandon the "hard line" upheld until a few weeks before by the Republican Administration of General Eisenhower. But the policy of the new government was no less reactionary and violent.

Actually, United States policy had become more and more aggressive since before the San José meeting. On June 11, 1960, the *Wall Street Journal* repeated that the government was supporting and backing the Cuban counterrevolution with the idea of repeating what had been done to Guatemala some years before. Early in October, Foreign Minister Raúl Roa denounced preparations for an invasion at a meeting of the General Assembly of the United Nations. Toward the end of the same month, the *New York Daily News* disclosed that Cubans were receiving military training on United States territory. On December 31, Roa addressed the Chairman of the Security Council of the UN and once more denounced preparations for a "military intervention" and on January 4, the Cuban government insisted on the danger of an "imminent military attack," which the United States delegates firmly denied, even ridiculing the charges.

On April 15, 1961, the Cuban representative to the UN, grim and outraged, said to the Assembly: "At six o'clock in the morning . . . today, B-26 planes, built in the United States, bombed targets simultaneously in . . . Havana, San Antonio de los Baños, and Santiago de Cuba. . . . The attack occurred without warning, in a cowardly fashion. . . . The responsibility for this act of imperialist piracy rests directly with the government of the United States."[17]

Official United States reaction to the invasion was incredible. On the very day it occurred, Adlai Stevenson denied that the United States had anything to do with it, and without the slightest scruples gave assurances that the military planes which had landed in Florida a few hours before were Cuban government planes stolen from the island by the rebels. Stevenson's false version coincided with the one given that same morning by the Associated Press, which the Central Intelligence Agency (CIA), in turn, had attributed to the so-called Cuban Revolutionary Council of Miami. "All we know about Cuba," declared Pierre Salinger from the White House, "is what we read on the wire services." And, in an even more emphatic and cynical tone, Secretary Rusk stated: "The American people are entitled to know whether we are intervening in Cuba or intend to do so in the future. The answer to that question is no. What happens in Cuba is for the Cuban people themselves to decide."[18]

Three days later, President Kennedy was to acknowledge, with obvious displeasure, that his government had "armed, trained, financed, and launched" the mercenary invasion of Playa Girón; but, like his predecessors, Theodore Roosevelt, Taft, and Coolidge, he, too, defended the unilateral "right of intervention" of the United States in the affairs of other nations. Throwing overboard the principles of the UN and OAS charters, he threatened Latin America, declaring arrogantly: "If it should ever appear that the inter-American doctrine of nonintervention simply conceals or excuses a policy of inaction, if the nations of this hemisphere do not fulfill their obligations against the penetration of Communism from outside, I want it clearly understood that this government will not hesitate to meet its obligations . . . assumed for the safety of our own nation."[19]

The Bay of Pigs attack once more exhibited the true meaning of United States foreign policy and revived a phase everyone had thought was dead; but at the same time the attack made it evident that the days when a few Marines or a small mercenary army could decide the fate of a country belonged to the past. In less than seventy-two hours, the Cuban people made a shambles of the invasion and the revolution passed another hard test and won the international allegiance it had been unable to win before. But its enemies would not accept defeat and returned to the attack without delay. The Bay of Pigs fiasco hurt them; Cuba emerged strengthened. The people of Latin America began to watch events in the Caribbean with increasing interest and, faced with an unrest and discontent which could easily grow into something far more serious and even get out of hand, the governments of America decided to meet at Punta del Este in August, 1961, to approve the program baptized with the name of the "Alliance for Progress" by President Kennedy some months before.

The "Alliance" was born amidst the enthusiasm of the heads of the American governments, who believed that they had at last found an effective response to the growing influence of the Cuban Revolution, to the discontent among broad sectors of the population of the continent, and to the phantom of international Communism. Faced with social revolution, the foreign ministers of America offered a formula of gradual evolution, of institutional reform, and of palace revolutions. Two important documents came out of the Punta del Este meeting: the Peoples' Declaration, and the Punta del Este Charter. The first promised to improve and strengthen democratic institutions, accelerate economic and social development, stimulate land reform, assure fair wages, abolish illiteracy, modernize tax systems, and proceed with the integration of Latin America. The Charter established the objectives and methods of the Alliance, indicating that the estimated minimum growth in per capita income of 2.5 percent per year would be achieved through development programs, economic integration, stable prices for basic exports, and some agrarian, fiscal, educational, and public-administration reforms.

The determined effort from the start to present the Alliance for Progress (ALPRO) as an unprecedented revolutionary event was very significant. For several months, especially in 1961 and 1962, the United States Coordinator, Teodoro Moscoso, kept repeating throughout America that the ALPRO was the most important revolutionary instrument the peoples of Latin America had ever had in their hands. Of course, it was evident that the Alliance involved a change and pre-supposed the acceptance on the part of the United States of certain old demands of the Latin-American governments; but it was just as obvious that it was by no means a revolutionary solution capable of transforming the socio-economic structure of Latin America. The Alliance was, no doubt, a new weapon —to be used, however, within the framework of the old anti-Communist strategy. At Punta del Este, the foreign ministers set forth the real problems and failures of Latin-American development, often making accurate diagnoses. However, they failed to resolutely confront the problems, to resolve to over-come the basic obstacles to progress and to call a spade a spade; the keynote was empty rhetoric, stereotyped phrases, and tempting offers which did not suffice to conceal that the governments of the continent, fearful of the possibility of real revolutionary change, were trying to protect their interests by means of superficial adjustments which would not seriously affect them.

José Figueres (President of Costa Rica, 1953–1958) made this significant statement: "We consider this Alliance a real-istic defensive measure on the part of the United States gov-ernment . . . in the protection of her liberties and with a view to her own interests." Dean Rusk declared: "The Alliance constitutes a concrete part of an indivisible whole . . . it rests on the concept that this hemisphere is part of Western Civil-ization which we are pledged to defend." Teodoro Moscoso, less given to subtleties and refinements, stated soon after: "In supporting the Alliance, members of the traditional ruling class will have nothing to fear." He added that privileged groups "must choose between the objectives of the Alliance and exposing themselves to the destructive type of revolution of a Fidel Castro." And, Rómulo Betancourt, whose adherence to the anti-Communist cause and imperialism was always rec-ognized and appreciated in Washington, said, in reference to the role of the Alliance, "We must help the poor . . . in order to save the rich."[20]

The success of the Alliance appeared increasingly remote even as early as a few months after the approval of the resolutions at Punta del Este, when the Alliance had barely been launched. Paradoxically, the only country actually carrying out the changes demagogically discussed at the Meeting of Foreign Ministers was Cuba, and it was looked upon with ever growing hostility. Even the government of Brazil, which was trying to realize certain institutional reforms in a modest and cautious way, became the target of the criticism of United States investors and officials. One thing it would have been difficult to foresee was that the United States government would charge interest on its loans even before the Alliance dollars arrived at their destination. In fact, in order not to leave even the pleasant memory that Punta del Este was the place where, for the first time, Latin America was offered significant cooperation in promoting its development, that famous Uruguayan spa was selected as the site of another inter-American conference: the seventh Consultative Meeting of Foreign Ministers, at which the governments of the continent resolved to confront Cuba once more.

The ostensible origin of the second Punta del Este conference was a speech by Fidel Castro in December, 1961, in which he declared that his country's revolution was a socialist revolution and that he himself was a Marxist-Leninist. Castro's declaration created a scandal in Washington. The delegate to the OAS Council from Colombia quickly proposed that a consultative meeting be called in accordance with Article 6 of the Rio Treaty. The majority of the countries accepted the proposal—no doubt under United States pressure. Some, however, abstained, and Mexico voted resolutely against the plan to call the meeting, claiming, with thorough justification, that "the convocation had no legal grounds" because there had been neither aggression, conflict, nor any other event that violated the territorial integrity, sovereignty, or independence of any American country, or which endangered the peace of America.

Nevertheless, a few weeks later, at the eighth Consultative Meeting of Foreign Ministers at Punta del Este, Mexico played an entirely different role from the one she had played with such dignity in Washington. Instead of confining herself to insisting that Article 6 of the Rio Treaty was inapplicable and that the sanctions provided in Article 8 of the same treaty could not be imposed upon Cuba for that reason, Manuel Tello, President of the Mexican delegation, yielded to United States pressure and, abandoning basic legal and political principles for reactionary and formalistic legalism, said:

> For the first time in the history of America, one of our governments clearly states that it has nothing to do with what has up to now been the common denominator of the characteristic institutions of the New World. Thus, it seems that a radical incompatibility undoubtedly exists between belonging to the Organization of American States and the profession of Marxist-Leninist principles, as it would be in the case of avowal of the doctrine of absolute monarchy. . . . Membership in our organization is irreconcilable with the adoption of a system of government whose characteristics are not those of the representative democracies.[21]

The "Tello Thesis" which the government of Adolfo López Mateos (President of Mexico, 1958–64) took to Punta del Este was not original; it was, in essence, the Monroe Doctrine, which more than a century before had declared the political systems of Europe "incompatible" with those of the New World. It was General Marshall's thesis in Bogotá and Secretary Herter's in San José, Costa Rica in 1960, where he had asserted that "the inter-American system is incompatible with all forms of totalitarianism." The only contribution of the Mexican delegation was that it applied the principle to a concrete case—the consideration of the revolutionary government of Cuba as a "totalitarian" regime—thereby providing the ministers with a pseudo-legal basis for enabling them to vote the exclusion of Cuba without undermining the Rio Treaty.

The second Punta del Este conference was another victory

for Monroeism and McCarthyism. Just as, at Caracas and San José, the Latin-American foreign ministers had paid the price of their subordination and weakness, here they again allowed the caprice of a powerful country to take precedence over principle and to undermine the right of self-determination. The thesis of incompatibility was contrary even to the Bogotá Charter and, of course, to the San Francisco Charter, because it stripped the peoples of America, in the full exercise of their inalienable sovereignty, of the possibility of constructing their own social and political systems as they saw fit.

As one commentator said:

> Never had falser and cruder reasoning been put forward. In which law of the United Nations or of the OAS is such an absurd principle of incompatibility set forth? To condemn a country because it adopts, in full liberty, a system it prefers . . . is this not to violate its free self-determination?
>
> A resolution of such gigantic diplomatic, legal, and social senselessness could have been adopted only at a meeting of lackeys. But the deed remains recorded in the Final Act of that infamous Meeting of Foreign Ministers. Some day, the people— not only the Cubans—will rise up to denounce such ignominy before the tribunal of history.[22]

While the foreign ministers were preparing to expel Cuba from the OAS for not being a "representative democracy" like those of Somoza, Prado, Stroessner, or the United Fruit Company, the Cuban people approved the Second Declaration of Havana at a gigantic, truly democratic public meeting. Fidel Castro referred to the words Martí wrote to his friend Manuel Mercado: "I lived inside the monster and I know its entrails." And, referring to the seventh Consultative Meeting at which the Cuban Revolution had once again been condemned by imperialism and its subservient oligarchies, the Declaration stated:

> Cuba did not speak for the benefit of the foreign ministers . . . it spoke for the people and for history, where its words would find an echo. A great ideological battle between the

Cuban Revolution and Yankee imperialism was waged at Punta del Este . . . Cuba on the side of the people; the United States in favor of the monopolies. Cuba spoke for the exploited masses; the United States for the oligarchical interests . . . Cuba for bread; the United States for hunger. Cuba for equality; the United States for privilege . . . Cuba for the future; the United States for the hopeless past . . . Cuba for peace; the United States for aggression . . . Cuba for socialism; the United States for capitalism.

At the second Punta del Este meeting, it was clearly established that the intention of the United States was to block not only Cuba but also the other countries of the continent, which explains the adoption of unprecedented resolutions on "internal security" and surveillance that actually tended to limit the exercise of political rights.

The process of Latin America's subjugation to the designs of United States imperialism did not end at Punta del Este in February, 1962. The next episode took place in Washington and in Caribbean waters when, in October of the same year, President Kennedy unilaterally decreed the blockade of Cuba a few hours prior to a hasty and "informal" meeting of foreign ministers—who once more gave their authorization for the aggression, albeit with the timid reservations of two or three countries. The pretext was no longer the mere fact that Cuba had declared itself socialist and that this constituted a grave threat to America, but that it had installed "offensive weapons" on its territory—namely, long-range missiles. Once more, the weird logic of imperialism was evident: there are "offensive" and "defensive" weapons. As if the offensive or defensive nature of weapons depended upon their intrinsic qualities and not upon the objective fact that it is the policy of a country which is offensive or defensive! But facts mattered least. The important thing was to advance the fight against the people who had dared rebel against their master, a people who had rejected geographical determinism, political defeatism, and the thesis of "manifest destiny."

The weapons employed by the United States against Cuba were all "defensive," such as setting fire to sugar cane fields, constantly sending in saboteurs, an unremitting campaign of slander, the Bay of Pigs invasion, the unilateral blockade by the Pentagon, and the preparations for a new invasion. When Cuba, after reiterating that it had to arm itself in order to repel these aggressions, installed medium-range missile bases, it caused a scandal and immediate action: First the State Department and then the foreign ministers declared, unanimously this time, that the Cuban weapons were "offensive" and must be dismantled and removed without delay. The United States, with the very same type of weapons ready to enter into action, was not censured because its arms were "defensive." The only offensive weapons, according to the domesticated foreign ministers of the OAS, were those installed by Cuba on its own territory in order to confront imminent aggression by United States imperialism.

In 1962, the whole world, not just America, lived through days of fear and anxiety during the October missile crisis. The danger of thermonuclear war grew, pointing up the unbreakable link between peace and respect for national sovereignty. The United States decision to blockade Cuba in times of peace violated the principles of freedom of the seas, self-determination, and nonintervention; it further violated the OAS Charter by converting that body once and for all into an instrument by which a powerful country could impose its policy and interests upon those of the remaining twenty nations of the continent.

During 1963 and 1964, United States aggression multiplied behind the screen of "continental solidarity" and "common defense." The progressive measures adopted by Goulart's government in Brazil aroused the violent hostility of the United States. As a result, President Goulart was toppled and the constitutional regime with him, as had happened before with Getulio Vargas and Janio Quadros. Fear that leftist groups connected with FRAP [Popular Revolutionary Action Front] might triumph in Chile produced close surveillance over its political life and frequent illegal interventions. Violations by the CIA and FBI throughout the continent occurred frequently, and still another episode, even more violent than the previous ones, occurred in the effort to isolate Cuba from Latin America.

At the end of 1963, the Venezuelan government requested that the Council of the OAS convoke a meeting of foreign ministers to study and sanction acts of "intervention and aggression by the Cuban government." The Betancourt government denounced the alleged shipment of arms by a fisherman in the peninsula of Paraguaná as one of the main facts revealing the "offensive of international Communism." After the necessary red tape, the ninth Consultative Meeting of Foreign Ministers was finally held in Washington toward the end of July, 1964.

This meeting was obviously vital to the United States. The importance of reaching a unanimous agreement against the alleged Cuban aggression was stressed from the outset, with a view to applying the severest sanctions. It soon became evident, however, that unanimity was impossible.

The position of the United States delegate, Dean Rusk, was clear and unequivocal: "Faced with continued Cuban aggression, the moment . . . has come to let the Castro regime see that the American governments . . . will not tolerate any further their efforts to export revolution by means of the classical techniques of terror, guerrilla warfare, and the infiltration of arms and subversive agents. . . . Present ties between the government of Cuba and the countries of the Sino-Soviet bloc are *manifestly incompatible* with the principles and norms of the regional system." He accused Cuba of trying to destroy democracy in Venezuela and ended by stating: "Of course, this intervention cannot be allowed to go on without the imposition of sanctions."[23]

Cuba's answer to Venezuela's accusation was soon forthcoming. The Cuban government repeated that the charges were false and intended only to feed the campaign of slander and to pressure the few countries still maintaining relations with Cuba. There were reservations and disagreements at the meeting since several countries (Mexico, Chile, Uruguay, and Bolivia) considered that the Rio de Janeiro Treaty was not applicable and that the sanctions proposed by the United States and Venezuela were, therefore, not in order. In the end, however, a majority agreement was obtained, resolving to "sharply condemn . . . the government of Cuba for its acts of aggression and intervention against the territorial inviolability, sovereignty, and political independence of Venezuela."

The accusations were not really proved, it was not taken into account that Cuba was absent from the meeting and could not defend herself, the provisions of the UN Charter were not respected, and both the spirit and letter of the Rio Treaty were distorted by interpolating an odd form of "political aggression" which in no way affected the independence of Venezuela and much less the peace of the continent.

The Mexican delegate, Vicente Sánchez Gavito, said:

> Careful study has led us to the conclusion that it has not been demonstrated that either the inviolability or integrity of the territory or the sovereignty or political independence of Venezuela has been affected in any of the ways described in Article 6 of the Treaty. . . .
>
> The peace of Venezuela has not been broken, and the situation that existed there six months ago, which its government could control . . . did not represent, at any moment, a threat to the peace of the continent.
>
> The Rio de Janeiro Treaty is the one that places . . . the most serious obligations and responsibilities upon the American states. In it, as in no other, we have made a major surrender of sovereignty. We must use it, therefore, with extreme caution and deliberation.[24]

It is quite interesting to note that the Mexican delegate should have acknowledged that the Rio Treaty signified "a major surrender of sovereignty" inasmuch as, on the signing of the treaty seventeen years before, the opinions of several progressive thinkers like Narciso Bassols, who had said the same thing, were labeled intransigent, erroneous, and unfounded by the Mexican government.

The condemnatory resolution of the Consultative Meeting of Foreign Ministers received an immediate reply from Cuba. The day after its adoption, at an authentically public meeting of the kind never seen in the "representative democracies" of Latin America, the people and government of Cuba issued the Santiago de Cuba Declaration which denounced the aggressive campaign of the United States and other countries (the introduction of arms and mercenaries, violations of air space and territorial waters, provocations, slander, setting of repeated fires, acts of sabotage), stating that "it is an act of unprecedented cynicism that the accused should set themselves up as the judges to . . . impose illegal sanctions . . . which the Cuban people reject with indignation."[25]

The arbitrary imposition of sanctions on Cuba for aggressions she did not commit was not the product of a decision by the OAS to correct its former errors and become a zealous guardian of national sovereignty; it was simply another episode in the anti-Communist serial. Violations of sovereignty were permissible as long as imperialism perpetrated them, impelled by the force of its determination to defend its privileges in the so-called Free World. This was made evident several months before the condemnation of Cuba when a small country—Panama—proposed a Consultative Meeting to apply sanctions against none other than the United States itself for aggression.

On January 29, 1964, the Panamanian Foreign Minister, Galileo Solís, sent the following telegram to the Council of the OAS: "The Republic of Panama has been the victim of an unprovoked attack upon its territory and civilian population by the armed forces of the United States of America quartered in the Canal Zone, killing several Panamanians and wounding more than a hundred more, and creating a situation endangering the peace."[26]

This message was enlarged upon the following day by the Panamanian delegate to the Council, who said:

> During the incident, the Panamanian national flag was torn down and desecrated by the North Americans. . . .
>
> At about eight o'clock that night, the armed forces of the United States of America, stationed in the Canal Zone, went into action. . . . The inhuman attack of well-armed troops did not shake the patriotism of the Panamanians. The population, already inflamed by the brutal and unjustified aggression . . . formed new groups which insisted upon entering the Zone with Panamanian flags. The criminal action of war tanks and heavy arms turned it into an even more desperate situation . . . to which must be added the flagrant violation of the Panamanian air space by helicopters and planes of the United States Air Force flying at low altitude over the Capital. . . . The total number of victims of the aggression reached 21 dead and more than 300 wounded. . . .
>
> All of America will eventually understand what it means for Panama to be repaid with an attack for its conduct as an ally and friend; that a demand for its rights should have been answered with machine guns. . . . Panamanian students, who had nowhere to obtain arms, hit back with stones, as bullets sowed death around them. . . . And all this because they wanted to see the Panamanian flag waving over territory which is part of the Republic.
>
> What happened in Panama should make us stop and consider the future of continental solidarity. If force is what is to determine the solution of conflicts in the future . . . between our countries and the United States, we shall have buried the American juridical system forever.

The United States delegate, certain that no one would dare demand that the law be applied to the big aggressive power, completely ignored the grave event, and said:

> Mr. Chairman, I reserve my right to make a concrete statement at a future session regarding the details of alleged events referred to by . . . the representative from Panama. . . .

As President Johnson has said: "Our obligation to protect the Canal against riots, vandalism, sabotage, and other interventions, is based on the precepts of international law, business demands . . . and the necessity to guarantee the security of the Free World. These obligations cannot be abandoned. . . .

In short, Mr. Chairman, the United States rejects all charges of aggression.[27]

It sufficed at the ninth Consultative Meeting of Foreign Ministers for one government to fraudulently accuse Cuba of aggression because of arms discovered by a fisherman in an isolated place, for the defensive mechanism of the continent to enter into immediate action to condemn the alleged aggressor without even a hearing and without paying the slightest attention to its statement to the UN that the whole thing was false. In Panama, on the other hand, an armed attack by the United States upon a defenseless population, which left blood stains on the streets and machine-gun bullets in the innocent bodies of students whose only crime had been to demand that their own flag be raised beside that of the United States, was justified by the United States delegate as the result of supposed "business demands" and the obligations of his country to the Free World. This was sufficient to prevent the mechanisms for the defense of the independence and integrity of a nation from being utilized.

The people of Latin America learned a good number of lessons in 1964. It was made clearer than ever before that the source of aggression lay in United States imperialism and not in the Cuban Revolution.

Notes

[1] *Report of the Committee of Nine of the Inter-American Economic and Social Council*, Washington, 1962, p. 45.

[2] *Latin America and the Alliance for Progress*, by Alonso Aguilar, Monthly Review Press, April, 1963.

[3] E. Lieuwen, *op. cit.*

[4] *Memoria de la Secretaría de Relaciones Exteriores, 1958*, Mexico, 1959, p. 132.

[5] J. Gerassi, *op. cit.*, p. 225.

6 *Time*, June 23, 1958, p. 30.

7 "La Historia me absolverá," in *La Revolución Cubana* (discursos).

8 Cited in *La Política económica de la revolución cubana* by Alonso Aguilar, Mexico, June, 1959.

9 *Ibid.*

10 *Retorno a la Alborada*, by Raúl Roa, Havana, 1964, Vol. II, p. 260.

11 *Ibid.*, pp. 248, 254–256.

12 U.S. Department of State *Bulletin*, Vol. XLIII, No. 1107, September 12, 1960, pp. 396–397.

13 *Minutes and Documents*, Seventh Consultative Meeting, Washington, 1961, p. 318.

14 *Ibid.*, p. 408.

15 *Ibid.*, p. 323.

16 *Time*, August 22, 1960, p. 31.

17 Raúl Roa, *op. cit.*, pp. 452–543.

18 *The Invisible Government*, by David Wise and Thomas B. Ross, New York, 1964, pp. 61, 62.

19 *Política*, Mexico City, May 1, 1961, p. 3

20 Alonso Aguilar, *Latin America and the Alliance for Progress*, p. 31.

21 *Política*, March 1, 1962.

22 "Farsa concluida," by Ermilo Abreu Gómez, *Política*, February 15, 1962.

23 *Report on the Ninth Consultative Meeting*, Washington, 1964, p. 106.

24 *Ibid.*, (Doc. 47), pp. 2–3.

25 *Prensa Latina*, July 27, 1964.

26 *Tratado Interamericano de Asistencia Recíproca*, Vol. II, p. 219.

27 *Ibid.*, pp. 222–224 and 228–229.

10. From the Violence of Imperialism to Revolutionary Violence

The first Extraordinary Inter-American Conference held in Washington in 1964 was actually not very important, but it did constitute a further step in the subordination of Latin-American policy to United States demands. It was convoked to discuss the problem of the admission of new members to the OAS and a resolution was adopted, the Washington Act, which established that ". . . the interested state must sign and ratify the OAS Charter and accept the obligations of membership, particularly with regard to collective security, expressly mentioned in Articles 24 and 25 of the Charter." The same resolution authorized the Council to admit a new member with a two-thirds majority vote and provided that an application may not be passed upon while the territory of the country in question is involved in a dispute.

The debate on the system to be used in admitting new members to the OAS was revealing. Some delegations (Brazil, Costa Rica, the United States, and Ecuador) were in favor of specifically requiring ratification of the Rio Treaty as a means of bolstering continental defense. Other countries (Colombia, El Salvador, Haiti, Mexico, Nicaragua, Peru and others) proposed, and succeeded in putting through, an amendment which emphasized that new members of the OAS must accept "particularly, obligations related to collective security," a position which did not differ basically from the other one. The only country to disagree was Chile, which stated unequivocally that admission to the OAS could not be made subject to acceptance of the Rio Treaty, and that the Washington Act

131

extended the functions of the Council beyond the provisions of the Charter.

The resolution of the first Extraordinary Conference made clear, in the first place, the determination of many of the governments to make acceptance of the Rio Treaty a prerequisite to admission to the OAS and, in the second place, revealed the practically unanimous opinion that the supposed defense of America against Communism was of primary importance. In 1948, in Bogotá, a year after the signing of the Rio Treaty, no one would have accepted the idea that the OAS was essentially an instrument for the preservation of "collective security"; nor would anyone have accepted it in 1949 when, in accordance with a motion by Peru, it was considered expedient to link the OAS with NATO; and, it would have been even less accepted during the period of struggle against Nazism or even during World War II. But the Washington Conference made it clear that times had changed and that Cold War obligations were greater and more binding.

In 1965, however, Pan-Americanism was put to a final test which was to show up its true character more than anything else before.

On April 28, 1965, the government of the United States ordered the landing of Marines in the Dominican Republic. This unexpected military intervention caused consternation all over the world since the use of the Marines seemed to have been abandoned as an instrument of imperialist policy. The aggression was censured everywhere and even in Latin America itself various governments felt obliged to go on record as disagreeing with such a grave violation of the principle of nonintervention that had been so much discussed at the OAS before and after Bogotá.

The Santo Domingo episode exposed the true character of imperialism in the raw and thus provided a lesson which pointed up Latin America's dilemma today with such clarity that even at the risk of repeating what many readers will surely know, it seems important to summarize the key points of the Dominican tragedy.

• *April 24.* A popular movement (termed a "revolt" by the OAS) to restore the constitutional system and President Juan Bosch broke out in Santo Domingo.

• *April 25.* The *de facto* regime of Donald Reid Cabral fell and with the support of the constitutionalist movement, Dr. Rafael Molina became provisional President.

• *April 26.* General Elias Wessin of the military government gave the order from the San Isidro base to bomb a sector of the capital.

• *April 27.* President Molina restored the Constitution of 1963 and dismissed General Wessin, whose forces had bombed the city a second time. In Washington, President Johnson declared: "We are waiting for the Dominicans to restore order and to settle their internal problems."

• *April 28.* General Wessin announced the formation of a Military Junta. President Bosch declared from Puerto Rico: "Wessin's forces do not control the city" and "public opinion is against Wessin." Meanwhile, the OAS representative of the overthrown Reid Cabral government was stating in Washington that the popular movement, already victorious, was "the realization of Communist plans to make a second Cuba of the Dominican Republic."

The same day, a UPI cable said: "Wessin's forces could have crushed the uprising if it had only the military to deal with . . . but it could do nothing against thousands of civilians."

Toward 9 o'clock that night, when Wessin's failure was already known, Lyndon Johnson announced the landing of 400 Marines in Santo Domingo to "protect the lives of United States citizens." The "Johnson Doctrine" in action again.

• *April 29.* United States soldiers installed themselves in the San Isidro base, general headquarters of the anti-constitutionalist movement, thereby arousing sharp criticism from the first moment. Several countries called for a consultative meeting of the OAS; President Leoni of Venezuela sent Johnson a message saying: "I have been surprised by the news that United States forces . . . have landed on Dominican territory, which constitutes a violation of the principle of nonintervention." The Peruvian Minister declared that the intervention was "the most severe blow inflicted upon the inter-American juridical system in recent years." Even *The New York Times* pointed out that "the presence of United States Marines in Santo Domingo had no justification."

• *April 30.* At 2 A.M., the State Department announced that "the mission . . . of the Marines . . . is to protect United States nationals and foreigners whose lives are in danger," and that two battalions of the 82nd Paratroop Division had been sent out to reinforce the Marines, numbering 1,700 at this point. The *Jornal de Brasil* wrote, in reference to the intervention: "This is the end of the OAS."

• *May 1.* The AP reported that the forces under Col. Caamaño were not Communist.

• *May 2.* The United States forces reached a total of 14,000 men. Johnson declared that "the Communists [have] taken over the Dominican rebellion" and the purpose of the United States was "to prevent the establishment of another Communist state in the hemisphere."

• *May 3.* United States forces started to take action openly on the side of General Wessin and the anti-constitutionalist soldiers. The Mexican representative denounced the intervention as a violation of the OAS Charter. The UN Security Council took the Dominican case under advisement and while the Soviet delegate censured the intervention, Stevenson asked that the matter be left to the OAS Council.

• *May 4.* Col. Francisco Caamaño was named Provisional President and asked the Latin-American countries to recognize his government. The Uruguayan Senate unanimously condemned the United States military intervention.

• *May 5.* The Santo Domingo Act was signed and a cease-fire agreed to. Bosch denounced the aggression of the United States, and Averell Harriman, in Brasilia, declared that the "Dominican Revolution . . . was distorted by interference from Communists well-trained for terrorist action in Russia, China, and Cuba."

• *May 6.* Thanks to a maneuver which even permitted the former representative of the fallen Reid government to vote, the tenth Consultative Meeting approved (by the minimum vote required by the Charter) the creation of an inter-American force which, in the guise of a "multilateral intervention," was nothing but a cover-up for the United States aggression. Five countries opposed it and one abstained. The OAS resolution read:

> WHEREAS; The formation of an inter-American force will mean, *ipso facto*, the transformation of forces now on Dominican territory into a different force which would not belong to any one state or group of states but to an interstate body like the OAS, the Tenth Meeting . . . RESOLVES: To request land, naval, air or police contingents with which to form an inter-American force . . . whose purpose will be to insure the operation of democratic institutions [in the Dominican Republic].

The crude expedient of converting unilateral intervention into a "collective" action fooled no one. The measure was sharply criticized everywhere. In Mexico, a group of well-known intellectuals declared: "We denounce and condemn . . . the diplomatic maneuver hatched in the OAS Council aimed at transforming what was originally an intervention by the United States alone into a collective intervention, inasmuch as . . . it is even more serious to add the complicity of other states to the unilateral action in violation of the principle of nonintervention." Even in the United States a large group of specialists in Latin-American affairs protested against the military intervention, saying: "We condemn this act because it violates the principle of nonintervention . . . because it contradicts the loftiest aims of the Good Neighbor Policy . . .

and because it discourages and is antagonistic to democratic forces in Latin America."

The best proof that the step suggested by the United States was basically repudiated, even by the weak governments which dared make no open or formal objections, was that the supposedly inter-American force was nothing more than the United States Army, whose troops numbered 40,000 within a few days, under the command of a Brazilian general.

The second report of the Special Committee of the OAS in the middle of May stated that "the inter-American armed force . . . has not yet been actually formed because, to date, only the governments of Costa Rica, Honduras, and Nicaragua have responded to the call with troops consisting of 21 police, and 250 and 166 soldiers, respectively. . . . These forces will soon be swelled with 3 officers offered by the government of El Salvador."

• *May* 7. At the opening in Mexico of the Eleventh Period of Sessions of ECLA, President Gustavo Díaz Ordaz of Mexico declared: "The people and the government of Mexico are united in the conviction that it is for the Dominicans and the Dominicans alone to determine their form of government and their future, in general, without interference, direct or indirect, open or covert from outside."

• *A few days later*, the Mexican delegate, as well as the delegates from Chile, Uruguay, and other countries, censured the creation of the inter-American force as politically inexpedient and legally in violation of the OAS Charter and the Rio de Janeiro Treaty.

• *May 14*. The UN Security Council decided to take up the Dominican problem and to send a representative to study the situation at first hand.

• *May 19*. The ambassador of the constitutional Dominican government, Rubén Brache, denounced the military intervention and United States policy before the Security Council and indicated that Ambassador John Bartlow Martin "suggested" the idea of forming the junta with General Imbert.

Brache accused Martin of committing serious crimes with United States support, saying: "I declare that none of this would be happening if United States Marines had not landed in Santo Domingo. The government of the United States of America has lost its self-respect and the right to speak in the name of democracy and liberty."

• A *few days later*, in Mexico, Jesús Silva Herzog made a similar statement: "There would already have been peace in Santo Domingo for several weeks if the violent and unreflecting . . . President Johnson had not committed the error of intervening unilaterally with his Marines and paratroopers and if the OAS had not lent itself as an accomplice of this aggressor. The OAS, the poor OAS, has lost all of its prestige for the American peoples, and has sunk into the mire, the mire of infamy."[1]

The United States aggression against the Dominican Republic aroused understandable alarm and repudiation throughout the continent, and made it impossible to hold at that time the second Extraordinary Inter-American Conference, which the government in Washington had decided to use as a means of consolidating the "gorillarchy" of Castello Branco in Brazil. The conference, originally planned for May, could not possibly take place while the United States Marines occupied the Dominican base of San Isidro: To have tried to hold it at that moment would have been dangerous and perhaps even mortal for the OAS, and postponement was deemed the wisest procedure. The vital thing was to prevent the triumph of the Dominican people and to allow a little more time to pass, since the unexpected incursion by the United States had nullified the work of many months of preparation for the conference.

Nor was it possible to convene the conference in August. The gaping Dominican wound continued to bleed, and reservations concerning the plan of creating an inter-American military force were still manifest. A new date had to be set and, in the meantime, the sword had to be kept dangling and the threatening tone maintained. After all, the Johnson Doctrine was in the ascendancy. Any attempts to open new avenues of understanding and negotiation were superfluous flirtations with justice, common sense, and reason. The United States government seemed prepared to proceed on its own, alone and with no friends, and even to transform its abuses into alleged and strange "legal" principles of a new anti-Communist policy. On September 20, 1965, the House of Representatives approved, by a 312 to 54 majority, Resolution 560 which established the "right" to intervene in the internal affairs of another country, even by force, against the threat of Communist subversion.

The author of this measure was Representative Armistead I. Selden of Alabama, none other than the Chairman of the House Subcommittee on Inter-American Affairs, for whom an event like the uprising in the Dominican Republic implied a "violation of the Monroe Doctrine." Some Representatives (Donald Frazer, for example) labeled the resolution "contrary to the spirit of the OAS and UN Charters," and numerous Latin-American organizations objected to it indignantly.[2] *El Tiempo* of Bogotá published an editorial which said: "We do not wish to conceal the gravity of a resolution which validates the intervention of that country [the United States] in the politics of the nations of America." Another Colombian publication, *El Espectador*, considered the resolution "an offense against the free self-determination of peoples." And in the Peruvian Chamber of Deputies it was referred to as "a return to the imperialist policy of the United States."

The Selden Resolution, which undoubtedly served to enhance the already aggressive Johnson Doctrine, symbolized the end of another phase in inter-American relations. Under the influence of Cold War policy, national sovereignty had often been seriously infringed, but the adoption of the Selden Resolution implied a definitive abandonment of the principle of nonintervention which had been solemnly accepted in Montevideo and Buenos Aires three decades earlier and which, in 1948, had been formally raised to the rank of a norm of the inter-American juridical system.

From then until the opening of the Rio conference, the tone of United States policy was openly aggressive and once more revolved around the alleged need to strengthen the continental defense mechanisms without delay. From November 8 to November 12, 1965—on the eve of the Rio meeting— the sixth Conference of American Armies was held in Lima after the military chiefs of Brazil and Argentina, Arturo da Costa e Silva and General Juan Carlos Onganía, had announced their decision to "establish contacts between the two military forces for coordinated action 'against Communist penetration.' "[3]

The Lima accords were kept secret, and as on many other occasions, no one was able to determine precisely their scope or significance. But some isolated opinions, gathered by international news agencies, indicated the kind of climate that prevailed at the meeting. For example, General Giral Morzal of the Peruvian delegation declared, "Mutual anti-Communist defense pacts are indispensable for planning and coordinating military action and war efforts at the continental level." In Caracas, General Ramón Florencio Gómez flatly stated: "The armies are considering further action and the coordination of measures and procedures to be employed in the war against subversive repression."[4] The Rio conference had just started when the Inter-American Security Commission reported on "the intensification of Communist activities," and the general opinion was that the most important topic on the agenda would be the creation of an inter-American military force.*

At the second Extraordinary Conference of the OAS, diplo-

---

* Two days before the meeting, a Mexican newspaper had described the attitude of United States officials as follows: "The suspicion is confirmed that the United States has no other purpose than to bring pressure to bear to establish the so-called Inter-American Peace Force as a permanent body" which would only constitute for Latin America "a unilateral instrument made up of United States Army troops with no other mission than to crush any attempt at self-determination with violence."—*El Día,* November 15, 1956.

matic pressures, fears, false hopes, demagogic boasts and displays, cowardice, frustration, and disillusionment were once again the order of the day. As at previous meetings, the theme of democracy and defense against Communism monopolized the attention of almost all the delegates who, instead of raising their voices and protesting vigorously against the United States aggression in Santo Domingo, demanded new and more expeditious security mechanisms for the hemisphere.

In the midst of one of the severest crises of the OAS, when the jails of Brazil were overflowing with political prisoners and hundreds of distinguished Brazilians were seeking asylum anywhere possible to escape the violence and protect their most precious civil rights, General Humberto Castello Branco said at the opening of the conference: "We are here for another important step in Pan-Americanism. . . . We are today confronting far more subtle forms of aggression through *infiltration* and *subversion*. . . . It is imperative that we reconsider the concepts *aggression* and *intervention*. The first should not only be applied to conventional manifestations of armed power, but . . . to guerrilla warfare and psychological warfare.

"We do not need . . . lessons in democracy. We have succeeded in preserving it, without asking anyone for help, from imminent destruction at the hands of totalitarianism and we are engaged in the great task of democratic renovation."[5]

Encouraged by the audacity and cynicism of the Brazilian military, the representative of Stroessner of Paraguay, flaunting his total subordination to United States policy, said: "We believe that there should be a single leadership, something akin to a sole command for all the entities, counsels, and bodies of the Association. . . .

"We feel that we are active members, ready to cooperate in the great enterprise of strengthening representative democracy on the continent."[6]

Thus, the Rio meeting turned into a showcase in which the representative democracies of the continent were exhibited one by one to leave on record proof of their rare virtues. Ortega

Urbina of the Nicaraguan dictatorship of Somoza, shamelessly said: "The government of Nicaragua . . . is an eminently democratic government which grants all Nicaraguans the full use of all their freedoms regardless of their political coloration."[7]

And the delegate from the Haiti of grim Duvalier, sententiously added another admonition: "The Haitian delegation believes it advisable to reconsider the meaning of democracy as 'the government of the people, by the people, and for the people' in the light of the rich experience of the Haitian nation."[8]

To wind up this extraordinary democratic parade, the United States delegate, Dean Rusk, appeared on the scene with a new and disquieting thesis regarding democracy:

> We must examine *coups d'états* not in general terms but in particular, case by case. . . . In 1962, we declared Marxism-Leninism to be incompatible with the inter-American system. What we are now doing is giving the citizens of the Dominican Republic the opportunity of choosing a government that should not be either Trujillista or Castrista. . . . Since the tragic history of the Dominican Republic . . . we know that the task will not be an easy one. However, our mission is in accordance with the loftiest values and objectives . . . of the inter-American system.
>
> In the case of the Dominican Republic, the Inter-American Peace Force contributed decisively to preventing unnecessary bloodshed, as well as to creating conditions necessary for the Dominican people to decide their own future by means of votes and not of arms.[9]

A few months later, the Dominican people, under close surveillance by the OAS and the persuasive presence of the guns of the United States Marines, were indeed to decide "freely" their future, as foreseen by Rusk, by "votes" which it was easy to predict would be cast in favor of the former Trujillista, Joaquín Balaguer. And, recalling the Dominican crisis, the indulgent Secretary of the OAS, José A. Mora, was to endorse proudly Rusk's words by saying: "The dynamics of the inter-American system have provided obvious proof of its ability and effectiveness in this unfortunate emergency."

Despite the "dynamism" of the system, it was impossible at the Rio de Janeiro meeting to decide on the creation of a permanent military force. As a reward for Latin America's reasonable attitude, the United States government postponed consideration of the project, aware that conditions for approval were not yet ripe and that it was preferable to delay a few months while awaiting wider support.

Washington's policy, however, did not really suffer a defeat. "Latin American countries yielded in a matter of principle in exchange for the withdrawal of a project which the United States could not present without provoking a violent resurgence of the OAS crisis."[10]

Several countries took positions somewhat less weak than that of the majority. The Colombia delegation was the only one to censure United States intervention in Santo Domingo, but its proposed resolution—to accept collective intervention of the OAS rather than the unilateral intervention of one country in the affairs of another—was not even discussed. Mexico, Chile, and Uruguay opposed the creation of a permanent inter-American military force as well as the broadening of the powers of the Council of the Organization.

The Chilean Minister, Gabriel Valdés, declared:

> The inter-American system is looked upon with suspicion by the majority of the peoples of America, or, at best, is ignored as something foreign to its vital interests. . . .
> It is now intended to graft the so-called Inter-American Force onto this progressively weaker body. . . . The Inter-American Force would give a negative and dangerous ideological connotation to the system; it would destroy the fundamental principle of nonintervention and threaten to divide us into irreconcilable blocs. . . . [It would be] a dangerous graft which could bring about the demise of the organization.[11]

Antonio Carrillo Flores, head of the Mexican delegation, made a slick, evasive, and contradictory speech which, while coinciding in some ways with the old and respectable positions of Mexico's international policy, was obviously not intended to tackle any problem in depth. He declared: "My delegation cannot consent to lending its aid to permit principles such as nonintervention, prohibition of the use of force, and the legal equality of states to leave this Assembly weakened or impeded. . . .

"We cannot agree that without the solemnity of a treaty . . . international bodies should take upon themselves powers not granted by our peoples."[12]

Carrillo Flores was referring to the inadvisability of extending the powers of the OAS Council beyond those provided by the Charter of Bogotá, and, implicitly, to the attempt by various delegations to endow the system with new instruments of action, such as the Permanent Military Force.

It was revealing and disconcerting that, while the delegates' attention was centered on the question of the inter-American Military Force and the Dominican crisis, Mexico should have fostered—successfully, in the end—the creation of an Inter-American Assistance Fund, "to aid countries so requesting with food, medicines, and other articles . . . in emergency situations, whether resulting from natural causes . . . or social upheaval."

Basically, the Mexican position, though less obvious than others, was just as weak. Instead of taking the side of justice, Mexico voted in favor of a compromise without principle or possibilities. Instead of unity against a common aggressor, the criterion of unity with the enemy once more prevailed. The words of the Panamanian delegate, Fernando Eleta, left no room for doubt: "We would rather take no decision at all than one that will divide the nations. . . . Unity is now more important than anything else. If there is no agreement on a proposal, it is better not to submit it to a decision."[13]

Expediency once more prevailed over fundamental principles. The Latin-American governments did not go to Rio to defend and redeem the national sovereignty trampled upon in Santo Domingo, or to denounce the OAS as an instrument alien to Latin-American interests; they went to acquiesce, to seek, fruitlessly and without dignity, harmony with the aggressor while trying to bolster and prop the tottering inter-American system.

A distinguished Mexican journalist wrote:

> Wavering between fear and immediate political interests, America wishes to forget that today in Santo Domingo, tomorrow in another country, and the day after in still another, Uncle Sam's Marines will assume that all American soil is their own country and will overthrow or crown governments at their beck and call.
>
> Santo Domingo suffers its Calvary, dramatically, alone. As it has done before, Latin America offers the world the spectacle of suicidal disunity, absolute historical blindness, and shameful egotism. . . . Perhaps the worst tragedy of our continent, much worse than the wretched poverty, than colonialism and its consequences, is that pathetic blindness to common dangers and responsibilities.[14]

While the Rio conference was not a defeat for United States imperialism, neither was it a defeat for the Latin-American countries. Hardly had the curtain fallen on the production put on by the OAS in the Brazilian capital than the call for a Tricontinental Conference to be held in Havana in January, 1966, was announced. For the first time, important political organizations of the underdeveloped world—Africa, Asia, and Latin America—were to gather to get acquainted, to establish contact, to discuss common problems, and to try to join forces in the struggle they all were waging.

The Havana Conference was not an artificial gathering, a last-minute occurrence; nor was it a cunning expedient conceived by Fidel Castro to badger Pentagon or State Department advisers; rather, it was the fruit of long years of effort, and a tangible proof that the peoples of the three economically backward continents were finally beginning to become aware of their common interests and aspirations.

The road to the Tricontinental Conference had begun long ago. It had taken over a decade to come into being, having sprung from Asia and Africa and crossed the seven seas and five continents. Along the way were such milestones as the Manchester Conference of 1945 which had attempted, for the first time, to outline a global strategy for the African liberation movement; the Congress of Asiatic Peoples, held in India at the beginning of 1955; and the memorable meeting in Bandung in April of the same year at which the chiefs of twenty-nine Afro-Asian states vigorously defended the right of newly-liberated peoples to full independence and to the well-being which had been denied them for centuries. All these were symbols and ineradicable tracks on this road and the beginnings of an irreversible historical process, a process which included the Egyptian revolution, started in 1952; the nationalization of the Suez Canal, decreed in 1956; the long years of the bloody and heroic Algerian Revolution; and the ultimately victorious struggles of Kenya and Guinea. The road to the Tricontinental Conference was the way of the irrepressible national liberation movement that gained strength with the First Conference of African States in 1958, the triumph of the Cuban Revolution in 1959, and the Latin-American Conference for National Sovereignty, Economic Emancipation and Peace in 1961, which brought together hundreds of delegates from progressive organizations of the continent to examine jointly ways and means of confronting imperialist successes not only in Latin America, but also in Asia and Africa. From that moment, it was especially incumbent upon the Council of Afro-Asiatic Solidarity to advance the preparations for the Tricontinental Conference at meetings in Guinea, Tanganyika, Ghana, and Cairo; as it was incumbent upon Cuba, of course, to be the country generously offering its capital city for the historic reunion.

The Tricontinental Conference in Havana attracted the attention of the entire world. The fact that Cuba was its site, the unexpected and suspicious disappearance of Mahdi Ben Barka, Chairman of the Preparations Committee, a few weeks prior to its opening, the sharpening of the crisis provoked by United States aggression in Vietnam and the presence of its troops in Santo Domingo, as well as the fact that this was the first time delegates from Latin America, Asia, and Africa had assembled together, all contributed from the very start to arouse deep interest everywhere. Despite the meager coverage by the international news agencies, the debates were closely followed and the resolutions adopted were carefully analyzed in all corners of the globe.

From the first moment, there was no doubt that this was not going to be just another gathering at which deep-seated problems would be evaded or dealt with obliquely by seeking innocuous and insignificant accords. It was evident that statements in Havana were to be clear, frank, direct, and revolutionary.

President Osvaldo Dorticós of Cuba said:

> The countries gathering at this conference concretely and dramatically understand the meaning of "underdevelopment"; they know that it means economic backwardness, hunger, technical incompetence, illiteracy, disease, political oppression, exploitation of national wealth, domination by imperialism, direct or indirect, open or covert. . . . The ultimate cause of all the symptoms of underdevelopment is none other than the persistence of imperialist domination.
>
> No platform is better than this conference upon which to resolutely proclaim the right of peoples to oppose imperialist violence with revolutionary violence. . . . When imperialism and reaction close the doors to legal forms of struggle, it is a right and duty for people to answer armed violence . . . with revolutionary armed violence.[15]

For two weeks Havana echoed with the sound of many different languages spoken with a wide gamut of inflections but all ringing with the same note of yearning for liberation. The Tricontinental was not an ostentatious exhibition of cosmopolitanism designed to impress foreign ways upon the Cubans, nor was it a hackneyed bureaucratic event with prefabricated decisions. Deep-rooted national feelings among the delegates were joined with a determination to close ranks that transcended frontiers and local differences. While it is true that differences existed among the participants (prior to the conference itself, in almost all cases), in the end agreements were reached which undoubtedly represent progress in the struggle for the full independence of the backward nations of Latin America, Africa, and Asia.

The conference proclaimed:

—The right of access to modern technical knowledge.
—The right to the enjoyment of a healthy life.
—Full equality of all men and the duty to combat all manifestations of racism.
—The right to be free of foreign military bases.
—The right to political, economic, and social liberation.
—The duty to come to the aid of all peoples "involved in a national liberation struggle, or suffering imperialist aggression, anywhere in the world."
—The right to oppose imperialist violence with revolutionary violence.
—Solidarity with peoples who have had to resort to armed struggle in defense of their integrity or independence.

On economic questions, the conference proclaimed:

—The need to end the exploitation of man by man.
—The need for common struggle against imperialism.
—The need to speed up economic development, particularly through national control of basic natural resources, the nationalization of banks and other enterprises, state control of foreign trade and foreign exchange markets, and the broadening of the public sector and economic planning.

Regarding the OAS, the Havana Conference resolved that:

Since its proclamation last century, the so-called doctrine of Pan-Americanism arose in order to prevent the regional unity of Latin America and to reinforce the Monroe Doctrine anew. . . .

The Organization of American States has neither legal nor moral authority to represent the Latin-American continent. . . .

Governments emerging from liberation movements will not be obliged to respect the agreements . . . of the OAS and especially those which invalidate the principles of nonintervention, free determination, and sovereign equality of nations.[16]

It was further resolved to condemn the so-called Inter-American Peace Force. Concerning the struggle of Latin-American peoples, it was recommended that the revolutionary movements in countries where conditions were most critical examine their problems as a whole and join forces against the common enemy—and they were offered active solidarity to "counteract imperialist policy more effectively."

The Tricontinental Conference had certain shortcomings probably precipitated by the haste of the final months of preparation. Several Latin-American delegations were not sufficiently representative of anti-imperialist forces in their respective countries, nor did they work with the intensity, insight, and unity of spirit necessary to attract progressive and significant organizations and personalities. Analyses of the current activities of imperialism in Latin America and their relation to the ruling classes were often too general and schematic—and at times even nonexistent. Some of the speeches in the debates revealed obduracy and inability to find new avenues in the existing complex, changing situation, so filled with pitfalls and, in many aspects, dominated by the enemy. That the Sino-Soviet conflict should have intruded into various matters, as had occurred at other international meetings of anti-imperialist forces, robbed various decisions of their force and also constituted a factor which the enemy once more tried to exploit in order to sow confusion and discouragement. But, in spite of everything, it would not be an exaggeration to ascribe great historical importance to the Tricontinental Conference.

The central theme of the meeting was unmistakable. Its language was so direct and precise, the tone of the main protagonists so firm, the denunciations so forceful, and the determination to fight and win so manifest that the curiosity, interest, and attention shown by the governments threatened by the revolutionary slogans of the Tricontinental Conference in the early sessions soon turned into anxiety, irritation, protests, and understandable fear. The hard-hitting words of Osmany Cienfuegos could not but be received with concern by those who, obsessed with preserving their privileges, were trying to impede profound social change at all costs. Recalling a statement by Fidel Castro, Cienfuegos said: "The duty of all revolutionaries is to make revolution." He immediately added what was to become one of the great slogans of the conference: "This vast humanity has cried 'Enough' and has begun to move. Its giant's march will not be stopped until true independence is won. *Patria o Muerte! Venceremos!*"[17]

Understandably fearful of the revolutionary winds blowing from Havana, the Latin-American governments would not be stopped, either. On January 20, with the Tricontinental Conference barely over, the government of Peru called for a meeting of the Council of the OAS "to denounce a violation of the principle of nonintervention." The request coincided with an excited appeal from the former president of Colombia, Lleras Camargo, to reinforce "the struggle against subversion on the continent, and particularly against Cuba." A few days later, the United States Secretary of State, Dean Rusk, declared to the press that the Havana Conference had thrown into relief "Communist intentions of increasing terrorist and subversive activities on the Latin-American continent. . . . Many of the Latin-American delegates left the Tricontinental Conference, their suitcases bulging with money with which to finance and promote subversion."[18]

The same stale argument of "Moscow gold" was again brought into the act. It was to be expected that this should have been resurrected by Dean Rusk who once more assumed the main role in the anti-Communist offensive, though indiscreetly this time, behind rather transparent screens which were constantly revealing the hand of Lincoln Gordon or other State Department officials.

On February 3, with Chile and Mexico abstaining, the OAS Council passed a resolution emphatically condemning "the policy of intervention and aggression of the Communist states and other countries and participating groups" at the Tricontinental Conference, alleging that the Havana agreements and particularly the presence of official delegates from the USSR and Cuba, flagrantly violated the nonintervention Resolution No. 2131 adopted by the United Nations at its twentieth assembly on December 21, 1965. Some days later, based on the OAS Council resolution, a letter of protest was sent to the UN signed by the members of the OAS including Chile, which had previously abstained, but not by Mexico, Jamaica, or Trinidad-Tobago. The government of Mexico, in particular, maintained its abstention not so much for fundamental reasons but because it believed that the Charter of the OAS did not grant the Council powers to act on behalf of any member of the organization in dealings with other states or international bodies, such as in the case of the protest to the Security Council of the UN.

Cuba and the Soviet Union declared immediately that the delegates from their countries to the Havana Conference had not attended officially or as government representatives. Fidel Castro addressed a strong letter to the General Secretary of the UN which said:

> It is incredible that such governments should have the cynicism to bring accusations against Cuba and the Conference of Solidarity Among the Peoples of Asia, Africa, and Latin America. . . .
> With the cowardly and shameful complicity of those very governments, Yankee military occupation and the oppression . . . of the Dominican Republic are maintained. . . . It is indeed the height of cynicism that Mr. García Godoy . . . should sign that declaration in the name of the country, no less, which is occupied by Yankee troops and other foreign mercenaries. . . .
> The peoples under those governments have the right to sweep away, sooner or later, those treacherous governments at the service of foreign interests within their own countries. . . .
> To proclaim the rights of those peoples oppressed and exploited by imperialism with the complicity of the oligarchies . . .

does not constitute an act of intervention, but precisely a struggle against intervention.

It is incorrect to confuse independence with intervention.[19]

For several weeks, the most conservative newspapers of the continent used the Tricontinental Conference as a convenient pretext for emphasizing a grave threat hovering over each and every one of the countries of America. The demand to create efficient instruments of defense against Communism was constantly repeated; the Inter-American Force was brought up once again as well as the need for the OAS Council to be free to act untrammeled by delicate questions which were reserved by the Charter of Bogotá for the highest bodies of the inter-American system.

When a meeting of a special committee was called toward the end of February, 1966, to discuss those possible reforms of the OAS Charter which were to be proposed a few months later at the third Extraordinary Inter-American Conference, it was quite clear that the forces interested in turning the OAS into an even more docile instrument at the service of United States foreign policy would return to take up the offensive.

The United States proposed "empowering the OAS Council to mediate in controversies among countries of the continent even in cases when the interested parties would not voluntarily submit to such a procedure," and the creation of "a consultative committee of military representatives . . . which could be the Inter-American Defense Board."[20]

In Panama, however, as at previous meetings, disagreements and contradictions were soon to come to the fore. The Mexican delegate, Rafael de la Colina, said: "Mexico will refuse to give its vote to any proposal which tends to grant the OAS Council political powers beyond those which clearly and limitedly we have already granted it."[21] The Chilean Minister, Gabriel Valdés, declared; "I am optimistic, because I believe the conscience of Latin America and the United States is aware that the system as such cannot continue because it has lost its prestige."[22]

It was easy to see that two different positions confronted one another; on the one side, the governments wanting to endow the OAS with more effective means of combating "Communist subversion"; on the other, the nations which, though recognizing the "reality of the Communist threat," insisted on incorporating into the Charter of the Organization the principles of the Alliance for Progress and of the World Conference of Trade and Development which had been held in Geneva in 1964. Within a few days, the original and vague agreement of the majority of the Latin-America delegates regarding the problems of development became the first draft of a plan for reforms and additions to those articles of the Charter which contained certain measures tending to accelerate economic growth and to obtain more favorable conditions in international trade. But, unlike other meetings at which the United States accepted various economic demands in exchange for greater political subordination, this time, at Panama, the United States rejection was immediate and flat. The preliminary draft was criticized as "unnecessary," "too long and wordy," and "too far removed from the spirit of inter-American equality of the Charter." And, in a less conventional tone in which his annoyance was evident, Senator Jacob Javits explained his country's rejection by saying, "The United States cannot sign any old piece of paper handed it by the Latin Americans."[23]

While discouragement pervaded Panama and Buenos Aires (where there was at that time a meeting of the Inter-American Economic and Social Council at which the same flat rejection by the United States delegation was to be forthcoming), in Washington, April 14th was declared "Pan-American Day" and Congressman Armistead Selden exhorted the governments of the continent to strengthen the OAS, using the same vehemence with which he had proposed a resolution months before that raised intervention by one country in the affairs of another to the rank of a "right" of United States imperialism to trample the sovereignty of other nations. He declared: "I urge you to recognize that the ultimate objectives of the Alliance for Progress can only be attained if the OAS is ready to meet face to face the constant hostility emanating from the Communist bases in Cuba."

Congressman Dante Fascell, a southern colleague of Selden's, also exhibited his government's absolute lack of understanding of the problems of Latin America, as well as its proverbial ability to see spooks behind every bush, with his statement that the celebration of Pan-American Day in Washington "serves to demonstrate to Latin America that the United States is wholeheartedly on its side in the struggle against Communist usurpation."[24]

Between 1962 and 1966 alone—that is, during the first four years of the "decade of progress"—constitutional law and order in Latin America was broken from eight to ten times by military forces bent on combating Communism and assuring "representative democracy." Frondizi in Argentina; Ydígoras in Guatemala; Arosemena in Ecuador; Bosch in the Dominican Republic; Villeda Morales in Honduras; Goulart in Brazil; and shortly after, Arturo Illía in Argentina, were all to topple, one after the other, charged with ineptitude and leniency toward Communism. Their removal from office was a reflection of the hard line of Thomas Mann and others in the State Department, who advocated supporting Latin-American military dictatorships as long as they were Anti-Communist and protected United States investors.

While the last Panama Conference was in session, Senator William Fulbright, Chairman of the Senate Foreign Relations Committee, said in a speech at the University of Connecticut: "Possibly we weren't made to spread the gospel of democracy. . . . Possibly, it would be more advisable for us to concentrate on our own democracy instead of trying to impose our version of it on all those unfortunate Latin Americans who stubbornly oppose their northern benefactors instead of fighting the real enemy we so graciously found them."[25]

How right he was!

Notes

[1] The various quotations in this summary are mainly from: *Cuba*, June, 1965 ("Santo Domingo, Tierra de Lucha"); the Chronological Summary presented at the Tenth Consulative Meeting; *Cuadernos Americanos*, July-August, 1965; *Prensa Latina*; and *El Día* of Mexico.

[2] *Política*, October 1, 1965, pp. 29–31.

[3] "La Segunda Conferencia Interamericana Extraordinaria," by Pelegrín Torras, *Cuba Socialista*, January, 1966.

[4] *Ibid.*, p. 58.

[5] *Acts and Documents of the Second Extraordinary Inter-American Conference*, Vol. II, Doc. 44, Washington, 1965, pp. 2, 4, 5 and 6.

[6] *Ibid.*, Doc. 57, pp. 65 and 68.

[7] *Ibid.*, Doc. 68, p. 77.

[8] *Ibid.*, Doc. 56, p. 86.

[9] *Ibid.*

[10] Pelegrín Torras, *op. cit.*, p. 64.

[11] *Acts and Documents of the Second Extraordinary Inter-American Conference*, Vol. II, Doc. 83, pp. 159, 161.

[12] *Ibid.*, Doc. 69, pp. 105 and 114.

[13] *Ibid.*

[14] "¿Amigo de Todos? Amigo de Nadie," by Francisco Martínez de la Vega in *Siempre*, Mexico, December, 1965.

[15] "Primera Conferencia de Solidaridad de los Pueblos de Asia, Africa y América Latina," *Cuba Socialista*, Havana, February, 1966, pp. 33–35.

[16] *Ibid.*, p. 186.

[17] *Ibid.*, p. 77.

[18] UPI cable published in *El Día*, Mexico, January 26,1966,

[19] *Política*, February, 15 1966.

[20] *El Día*, February, 28, 1966

[21] *Ibid.*, March 24, 1966.

[22] *Ibid.*, February 26, 1966.

[23] *Ibid.*, April 3, 1966.

[24] UPI, April 7, 1966.

[25] UPI, Storrs, Connecticut, March 22, 1966.

11. Structural Changes, Progress, and Peace

For a hundred and fifty years Latin America has lived under the domination of foreign interests, its sovereignty alienated, and its principal sources of wealth in foreign hands. Monroeism, territorial expansion, manifest destiny, dollar diplomacy, Point Four, hemispheric solidarity, the struggle against international Communism, and the Alliance for Progress are not the expressions of fundamentally different policies but rather a series of names for the same old line of domination and plunder pursued on the continent to this day by the United States.

It would be difficult to evaluate precisely the amount of political, economic, and social damage that this subordination has brought the Latin-American countries, but it cannot be denied that it has been enormous and, in many cases, irreparable. Colonialism and imperialism have historically been the main obstacles to Latin-American development. During the century and a half of relative independence enjoyed by Latin America, the big Western powers, and the United States in particular, have smashed into its countries, violating them, deviating and arresting their development, irrationally exploiting their natural and human resources, subordinating entire nations to the mean and selfish interests of the big monopolies, more than once bathing their territories in the blood of criminal wars of conquest, mutilating their ancient cultures, and undermining the force of law to impose the law of force. Overpowering economic and diplomatic pressures have been brought to bear to support the outworn and backward in preserving their privileges, and to defend one

155

freedom alone—that of free enterprise, trade, and exchange; in short, the freedom to exploit people and wealth with no restrictions whatsoever and with unbridled license.

For the people of Latin America, imperialism has meant subjugation, exploitation, constant meddling in their internal affairs, violations of sovereignty, irretrievable draining off of their nonrenewable natural resources to the point of exhaustion, extraction of economic surplus which under other historical conditions would have served to accelerate their own economic development, and violation of the right of self-determination of every nation—the right to choose the political and social system it prefers.

Imperialist policy during the last twenty years, far from changing to a form favorable to the economically backward nations of Latin America has, on the whole, become an increasingly aggressive and insurmountable obstacle to progress. The government of Franklin Roosevelt, as we have seen, opened new prospects for change and progress for the inter-American system. Even though the United States continued to defend its interests and often the interests of its great international monopolies, the struggle against Fascism and the danger of war, and the alliance with the Soviet Union during the war, encouraged the democratic forces of Latin America at certain moments—and, between 1933 and 1944, provided Pan-Americanism with its most favorable period. Since World War II, however, United States policy has become more and more irrational until it has culminated in the monstrous Johnson Doctrine which is, at bottom, an attempt to use the mechanism of "hemispheric solidarity" to counter the exercise of national sovereignty. According to that doctrine, the expansion of Communism in Europe or Asia, and the triumph of the Cuban Revolution, are no longer the only dangers to the continent; so is the determination of a people to overthrow a military dictatorship, as happened in Santo Domingo. And all this is in the interests of imperialism—interests which are audaciously and skillfully equated by their defenders with those of "Western civilization."

World War II not only rescued the Western World from the depression that followed the 1929 crash, but it also gave an enormous boost to the United States economy which, from that moment on, was to reach unprecedented levels of activity and win a dominant position in the so-called Free World, such as perhaps no power had ever had at any previous stage in history.

If the socio-economic conditions in the United States had changed in accordance with the policies of the New Deal during its best period and if the anti-monopoly struggle begun in the thirties had succeeded instead of having been given up, as was finally the case, surely the course of events since World War II would have been different. The monopolies, however, not only survived, but grew and consolidated themselves, broadening their field of action both outside and inside the country, and subjecting Latin America and other economically backward areas more profoundly to their domination. At the same time, even as peace was being restored, they successfully imposed the Cold War policy, and with it their thesis that the maintenance of an enormous military apparatus by the United States was the only means of insuring prosperity for its economy and that of the West in general. The adoption of a policy of huge military spending both internally and on the Cold War abroad, logically became two inseparable halves of the same policy.

It was not difficult to find a pretext for the adoption of this policy; Churchill and Truman found it in the expansion of socialism and the development of national liberation movements. A new phase in the process of historical development became converted, within the context of the narrow and reactionary ideology of subservience to imperialism, into a "sinister conspiracy," a "criminal subversive attempt," a "grave danger to Western civilization."

Not even during the darkest years of Fascism and the war was United States policy so violent. This, in part, explains why Fascism destroyed everything—cities, countryside, factories, schools, illusions, works of art, innocent lives—but did not threaten the monopolies with extinction. Fascism was a modality, brutal without question, but in the final analysis only an aspect of imperialism to which United States monopolies were able to adapt themselves advantageously and without difficulty. Socialism and the national liberation struggles, on the other hand, spell the death of imperialism and the death of the "Free World"—a world in which the monopolies, in the name of the so-called free market, have enjoyed almost unrestricted freedom to exploit, enrich themselves, and rob the people of what belongs to them.

The defenders of the dying world pursue and attack what is not solely or even basically Communism, just as what they defend is neither freedom nor democracy. The target of their violence is any popular movement which tries to change the *status quo* or any action on the part of the people to recover their own wealth and become masters of their own destiny. It even includes any philosophy or objective scientific position which seeks to demonstrate the laws of historical process and to reveal that it is a lie that humanity's future offers either a life of servitude under abhorrent and unwanted totalitarianism or death in a nuclear holocaust. What they defend are not democratic freedoms; they violate them daily. What they actually defend are the markets of the great powers, the sources of cheap raw materials, the old spheres of influence, selfish interests, and unfair privileges.

In every period of history, the privileged sectors have stubbornly insisted on closing the door to progress and social change. The birth and initial development of capitalism was not a gentle or easy process. The new system had to destroy the old feudal order in order to impose itself, but the resistance being put up today against socialism and the liberation of nations which are at last breaking the chains of colonialism has perhaps no parallel in history. Incapable of organic change, of resolving its basic contradictions, or of offering humanity an outlook of peace and well-being, imperialism recklessly postulates: "War, not socialism! Death before social change! Progress and peace are incompatible!"

Today, one may or may not be in favor of socialism or support the national liberation of peoples who have not yet achieved full independence, but it is unforgivable to act like an ostrich by insisting that the awakening conscience of the people and the very laws of social development are merely the products of intrigue in Moscow, terrorism learned in Peking, or Fidel Castro's sinister machinations aimed at exhausting the patience of the irascible Pentagon strategists. It is unforgivable to think that social progress must be stopped by brute force, with invasions by the United States Marines in one place after another like a desperate and hysterical fire brigade trying to extinguish the revolutionary conflagration of our times by the use of violence.

We are living decisive hours in America. When Churchill launched his war of hate against socialism and the national liberation movements, many people thought ingenuously that America would be able to live in peace on the margin of the "Communist threat." But much has happened since then which makes it apparent that the policy of anti-Communism does not wait for its enemies to make themselves known; it invents them when necessary, creates them artificially, and converts them into mortal dangers to "Western civilization" and "representative democracy"—concepts which are used as advertising slogans to conceal unspeakable interests having nothing to do with civilization or democracy.

The thesis that socialism, or simply the adoption of an advanced economic and social policy, involves grave threats to civilization and peace is an irrational, unscientific—truly incredible—concept which has nevertheless wormed its way into the ideology of Pan-Americanism and which has unscrupulously been put to use more and more frequently since the victory of the Cuban Revolution. But the people are beginning to understand much that escaped them before, to recognize that socialism is not incompatible with democracy, nor national liberation with Western civilization. What is actually incompatible with democracy is imperialism and all that its system implies in every one of the Latin-American countries: poverty, backwardness, dependence, and political regimes of force which regard the people as their most dangerous enemy.

Two decades ago, when Guatemala attempted to transform and modernize her weak and backward economy, to free herself from the oppressive yoke of the United Fruit Company and to stop being a "banana republic," she threatened no other country. She was not a danger to the peace of the world —not even to her closest neighbor, Mexico. When first President Quadros and then Goulart tried to initiate land reform in Brazil and to restrict the exportation of capital by foreign investors, they did not threaten any country either. The ones who denounced these acts as dangerous were Lacerda, then governor of the state of Guanabara, the most reactionary Brazilian landowners, and the United States government—all of whom soon showed their hands when they publicly congratulated the military officers who carried out the *coup* that ended constitutional government. When the Cuban people overthrew Batista, when the revolutionary government decreed the nationalization of large United States enterprises, and when Fidel Castro said he was a Marxist-Leninist—in none of these cases was the peace or security of the continent endangered, though it was understandable how keenly the foreign interests which had had Cuba in their hands for more than half a century felt the threat to their hegemony in Latin America.

The recent course of Pan-Americanism, in large measure an expression of the imperialist trend of policy in Latin America, is disquieting. The phase in which possible military attack by an extra-continental power could automatically involve the nations in a military conflict alien to their interests has been superseded by resolutions which have been accepted weakly and without dignity by their foreign ministers under pressure from the United States. The thesis of the "incompatibility of totalitarianism" and "representative democracy" brought to Bogotá by General Marshall as one of the first contributions of Cold War policy to those countries, has since developed significantly. What was really incompatible as far as the OAS was concerned was not totalitarianism but the Guatemala of Arévalo and Arbenz and the Cuba of Fidel Castro. They were incompatible despite the fact that both countries represented two of the most genuine examples of democracy America has known in recent times. Incompatible with the OAS were, in fact, the progressive reforms which Brazil tried to carry out under the government of Goulart and the struggle of the Dominican people to re-establish and enforce the Constitution and the democratic freedom it guaranteed. Incompatible with the interests of the United States government and the monopolies was the democratic revolution in Bolivia as expressed in Paz Estenssoro. Both the repudiation of totalitarianism and the defense of true representative democracy are so far from really being the concern of the OAS that not a single one of its members requested the convocation of a consultative meeting to study the danger to the continent represented by the "gorillarchies"; not one of them has denounced the governments of Nicaragua or Guatemala, Venezuela or Colombia, or the dictatorial regimes in Ecuador, Brazil, and Paraguay; not one has requested that the OAS, in accordance with its Charter, put an end to the criminal violations by the United States in Santo Domingo.

The countries of America face a dilemma: either they resign themselves to living in poverty and backwardness, dependent upon other countries, working without hope and standing by as their wealth is siphoned off for the benefit of others,

or they decide to stand up, live with dignity, demand respect
for their rights, and courageously confront the obstacles im-
peding and deforming their development.

Economic development is not only a question of investments or of the use of new techniques; it is a process which
presupposes profound changes, blocked so far in Latin America by imperialism and the oligarchies serving it. If the Latin-
American countries are to industrialize rapidly and raise the
living standards of their people, they will have to carry out
structural changes which release productive forces, accelerate
the capital-formation process, expand foreign markets, mobil-
ize and activate their creative energies, and modify their
foreign-relations framework to make possible a fair and bal-
anced type of trade which will in turn foster speedy and independent development.

Structural changes are not easily made, however, since they
inevitably affect the interests of national sectors and foreign
investors who obtain multiple benefits from the existing situation. It would be naive, at this point, to think that the United
States and the privileged groups in the Latin-American countries oppose only Communist movements. Mexico's experience
in its revolutionary stage and that of Guatemala, Brazil, Cuba,
and particularly Santo Domingo, show that such is not the
case and that the margin for peaceful social and political
change is constantly narrowing.

This question is so important that it is worth stressing. Any
progressive national program that affects the interests of the
monopolies, or of the national bourgeoisie linked to them;
any real advance in land reform; any more or less serious attempt at planning which reduces the radius of action of "free
enterprise" and imperialism, which tends to replace anarchy
with a minimum measure of rationality, or which impinges on
vested interests in one way or another; any structural change,
in fact, which oversteps the innocuous and ineffectual limits of
the Alliance for Progress, will be stubbornly and even violently
obstructed by national and foreign ruling groups, by the social

and political forces which fear progress and know that their privileges will never be safe in a dynamic community determined to eliminate the factors producing backwardness.

It would be simple to renounce such changes and seek an easier and bloodless path which might reconcile clashing interests and avoid social conflicts and tensions. But it is only the superficial schemes of reformists like Teodoro Moscoso or Luis Muñoz Marín which are constructed around this possibility.

Changes are imperative and many of them can no longer be delayed. Latin America will be unable to achieve any progress worthy of the name unless it institutes a different agrarian structure; another system of distribution which liberates small producers from speculation and parasitism; an effective nationalist policy to rescue the lands, mines, industries, transportation, banks, and in general, the means of production still in foreign hands; a bold anti-monopoly policy; open and growing trade with all countries, particularly the socialist group; an independent labor and peasant movement; and at least a minimum of rational economic planning and true political democracy.

What makes Latin America's situation more difficult and pressing is that it is not only just such essential reforms and changes that the government of the United States, the ministers of the OAS and, particularly, the Johnson Doctrine consider "incompatible with representative democracy" but even the very historical process toward higher and more rational forms of organization of economic and social life.

In an address in honor of Narciso Bassols a few years ago, I summarized the situation in these words:

> The right of self-determination of peoples, the right to choose the form of government they prefer, the right of revolution against tyranny, and the right to full emancipation have been judged and condemned outside the law by most of the governments of the continent at both the ninth and tenth Meetings of Foreign Ministers. And the right which is inherent in the

very concept of sovereignty, which is consecrated by modern
institutions, and which no people can renounce, has been converted into a serious crime in the eyes of the Foreign Ministers
of the OAS, into an aggression against territorial integrity, a
threat to the peace of the continent, and into an action which
may even call for the individual and collective use of armed
force.[1]

The idea is frequently advanced that, given their present
status, Latin-American countries have no choice but to withdraw from the OAS. The problem is more complex and difficult than that. It is evident that the OAS has become an instrument of United States imperialism. The actual instruments, however, are the governments which increasingly di-
vorce themselves from their people and go to Washington
to pay tribute to their master and to receive instructions on
how to act at the first sign of popular unrest.

Latin America must choose the road it is going to follow
from now on, and this can be done inside or outside the OAS,
as it can be done inside or outside the UN. The thing that is
really important to understand is that the Pan-Americanism
of Johnson and the OAS is by no means the culmination of
what Bolívar envisioned before the Congress of Panama 150
years ago, but quite the opposite; and that imperialism is not
defending Western or any other civilization, but only its own
interests and its own hegemony which are indeed in danger
in countries where the people have launched themselves on
the conquest of their liberation.

To defend freedom and justice is one thing, but to support
anarchy and privilege is something quite different. Freedom
for the monopolies engenders the servitude and backwardness
of peoples. To set up Anglo-Saxon democracy as the model
for all nations to copy, when such a model was never realized
in Europe even during the competitive phase of capitalist
development, is to put progress in a strait jacket and, what is
even more unacceptable, to seek to condition the exercise of

sovereignty and the right of self-determination to suit the interests of a few big imperialist powers.

Democracy cannot be pressed into a static and inflexible mold. Anglo-Saxon or otherwise. The form that the political regime of any nation takes must be the fruit of its special conditions and traditions, of the development of its society, and the free choice of its people. The zeal of the OAS and the State Department in seeking to impose a supposed form of democracy as the only true, legal, and viable one is indeed touching; it demonstrates the irrationality with which Pan-Americanism has been seized since the anti-Communist Rio Treaty and, most of all, under the Johnson Doctrine. And if such a stereotype of democracy seems unacceptable, it is positively grotesque to confuse it with that rare species of "representative democracy" which is being forced upon Latin America at all costs; a "democracy" without the people and against the people which in reality represents only privileged and decadent minorities, reactionary military castes, illegally enriched officialdom, foreign businessmen of all sorts, to say nothing of a swarm of scabs, informers, witch hunters, secret police, FBI and CIA agents, and other "forces" upon which many "representative democracies" are based today and which the Alliance for Progress vainly tries to whitewash.

The problem confronting Latin America is a major one. It would be an error even to entertain the idea that it is merely an external problem and to consider imperialism as something harmful but organically outside Latin America's national life. To believe that would be tantamount to considering cancer merely a rash. Imperialism is far from being just an "exogenous variable"; should their interests appear to be threatened, the ruling classes within the Latin-American countries also fear change and social transformation regardless of its extent.

Thus it follows that notwithstanding the fact that isolated elements of those classes may play a positive and even an important role, it seems clear at this time that it will not be the bourgeoisie, or the old landed oligarchy, or the newly enriched groups connected with industry, commerce, or government, which can turn back or modify the course of Pan-Americanism and reconstitute the Bolivarian meaning of regional integration in opposition to the Monroeist and Johnsonian version.

It devolves upon the countries of Latin America to carry out this task. It is up to them to go over to the offensive and tear the noble old banners of freedom and democracy out of the hands of anti-Communist Pan-Americanism, to win full independence, to assure the continuity of the historical process, to defend true civilization, and as Martí said, to achieve "alliance with the whole world and not with just one part of it against another."

The words of General Lázaro Cárdenas in closing the Latin American Conference for National Sovereignty, Economic Emancipation and Peace, held in Mexico City in 1961, are already in the consciences of many Latin Americans and form part of the ideology of the revolutionary forces which are gaining ground from the enemy every day from Chile to Venezuela and from Peru and Colombia to the Dominican Republic:

> The new stage of liberation has commenced in Latin America. . . . We must put an end to the state of dependence which characterizes us today. . . . The fundamental force which blocks the development of Latin America is United States imperialism. Its close alliance with national oligarchies, the ruinous effects of its economic and cultural penetration brand it as the main cause for the general stagnation which prevails on the Latin-American scene.
>
> The defeat of imperialism is a fundamental condition for any development plan for our countries.
>
> We reject the Monroe Doctrine and the policy of alleged hemispheric security which undermines our sovereignty. Against an oppressive Pan-Americanism we propose a Latin-Americanism which will free our productive forces, broaden our possibilities for development, strengthen solidarity and cooperation among our peoples, and contribute effectively to peace in the hemisphere and the world.[2]

The struggle for total emancipation may be long and difficult. It will surely call for lasting and unstinting self-sacrifice, but just as surely will it end in victory.

Notes

1 "Vigencia del pensamiento de Narciso Bassols," lecture by Alonso Aguilar, July 30, 1964.
2 *Final Declaration of the Latin American Conference for National Sovereignty, Economic Emancipation and Peace*, March, 1961.

Note to Appendices

Two appendices follow, which we hope the reader will find of interest. The first presents, in extremely schematic form, the principal agreements adopted in the inter-American system throughout its history of roughly eighty years. The second presents a brief resume of the principal resolutions of the Latin-American Solidarity Conference, which convened in Havana in mid-1967.

Article 32 of the OAS Charter includes, among the organizations of the system, the Inter-American Conferences, the Consultative Meetings, and the Specialized Conferences. The first, which according to the Charter must be convened every five years, are the highest authority. Ten have been held so far; the last one met in Caracas in 1954. The Consultative Meetings of the Ministers of Foreign Relations—twelve in all—deal with urgent problems and frequently with questions of continental security. The Specialized Conferences convene on the initiative of the ordinary conferences or the Consultative Meetings, and deal with concrete matters of special interest. From them we have selected seven of the most important, held between 1936 and 1967.

The two appendixes presented here permit, among other things, an evaluation of two essentially different attitudes: that of the governments on the one hand, and that of the peoples on the other. The former has attempted—especially since the beginning of the Cold War—to restrain the struggle for a thoroughgoing social transformation; the latter has attempted to advance the revolutionary struggle.

Appendix I

Principal Meetings of the Inter-American System

Pan American Conferences

First Conference: Washington, 1889–1890

It was established that foreigners enjoy the same civil rights as the nationals of a country and that a country does not have to assume or recognize any obligations or responsibilities other than those established for nationals.

It was agreed to settle international problems and disputes by peaceful means. In principle, compulsory arbitration was adopted as the means for settling controversies, except in cases when the independence of any of the parties involved was endangered.

It was recommended that trade among the countries of America be encouraged, railway and maritime transportation be promoted, and an inter-American bank be created.

The International Union of American Republics was established, to be represented in Washington by a Commercial Office.

Second Conference: Mexico City, 1901–1902

With reference to the rights of foreigners, the recommendations made in the first conference were reaffirmed, establishing that in case of complaints or claims, suit should be brought before the competent court of the country and diplomatic channels should not be resorted to except when denial of justice was evident.

The question of arbitration was fully discussed and both a Treaty of Compulsory Arbitration and a Treaty of Arbitration on Pecuniary Claims were signed by all the nations in agreement.

It was agreed to reorganize the commercial office established at the Washington conference into an International Office of the American Republics which would function as the secretariat of the inter-American organization.

Third Conference: Rio de Janeiro, 1906

The principle of arbitration was ratified as being the most

169

suitable means of settling certain international disputes and it was recommended to the Second Peace Conference, held several months later at The Hague, that it re-examine the problem in order to arrive at an international agreement on arbitration. The so-called Drago Doctrine was thoroughly discussed and several countries attempted to have the use of force as a means of collecting a country's debts prohibited. Finally, the conference agreed to refer this matter, as well, to the above-mentioned meeting at The Hague.

Various monetary and foreign trade problems were also studied at this conference.

Fourth Conference: Buenos Aires, 1910

It was agreed to extend the life of the Treaty of Arbitration on Pecuniary Claims. In general, the recommendations on the use of arbitration made at The Hague meeting in 1907 were accepted. The Bureau of the American Republics was replaced by the Pan-American Union which was transformed into a permanent committee of the international American conferences.

Various problems regarding transportation and foreign trade were taken up, as was done in the previous conferences.

Fifth Conference: Santiago, Chile, 1923

A Uruguayan proposal to create a League of American Nations was discussed and finally rejected. The need for revising the operation of the Pan-American Union was insisted upon. The advisability of reducing military expenditures was brought up. It was proposed that certain international disputes be submitted to a special investigating commission which would function with the cooperation of the parties to the conflict through the Gondra Treaty (so called because it was proposed by Dr. Manuel Gondra, former President of Uruguay and chief of its delegation).

Sixth Conference: Havana, 1928

In view of the impossibility of preventing the United States from taking a direct part in the Pan-American Union, it was agreed that this agency should have no political functions. The problem of intervention was fully discussed in connection with the report presented by the Pan-American Meeting of Jurists (Rio de Janeiro, 1927). The majority of the countries present in Havana were in favor of the principle of nonintervention. However, in view of the refusal of the United States to concur, it was agreed that no formal resolution would be made on this topic.

Seventh Conference: Montevideo, 1933

A variety of topics was considered at this meeting. A non-aggression, anti-war treaty based on an Argentine proposal was adopted. The so-called Good Neighbor Policy of the United States was promulgated at this time. Tariff reductions were recommended (largely as a result of the passage of the Smoot-Hawley tariff in the United States). In particular, the principle of nonintervention was again fully discussed and the Convention on Rights and Duties of the States was unanimously adopted. It provided that "no State has the right to interfere in the internal or external affairs of other States."

Eighth Conference: Lima, 1938

The Lima Declaration was adopted and the principle of non-intervention was reaffirmed. In view of the prevailing international situation resulting from the advances of Nazism and the signing of the Munich Pact, the importance of American solidarity was stressed and, at the same time, it was agreed that each country should take the defensive measures it deemed necessary. It was also agreed that if the territorial integrity of any American nation were violated, various measures would be invoked to effectuate the solidarity of the others.

Ninth Conference: Bogotá, 1948

The Charter of the Organization of American States was adopted, thereby substantially modifying the legal structure and various other aspects of the Pan-American organization. The Treaty on Pacific Settlements was also approved, which from that time on was called the Bogotá Pact. An economic agreement was formulated which was basically a repetition of various pronouncements on foreign trade, foreign investments, and international cooperation dating back to World War II years. The basic problems of Latin-American underdevelopment were virtually ignored, and ultimately only the Bogotá Pact and the economic agreement were ratified by a few countries.

The conference also approved a Declaration of the Rights and Duties of Man and the famous Resolution XXXII on Preservation and Defense of Democracy in America which, strictly speaking, was no more than a violent explosion of anti-Communism and McCarthyism at the heart of the inter-American organization.

Tenth Conference: Caracas, 1954

At the height of the Cold War, the conference was used as an anti-Communist platform. The "Communist threat" to the hemisphere was the central topic of debate, and paradoxically, the only support the United States delegation was able to win for its theatrical and hypocritical gestures in favor of freedom was the far from unanimous and unconditional backing of the most brutal of the Latin-American dictatorships. Mexico and Argentina suffered serious setbacks vis-à-vis the Caracas Declaration which fundamentally again nullified the principle of self-determination of nations, and Guatemala, which was branded the red sheep of the Pan-American flock because of its democratic revolution, vigorously opposed that Declaration.

Special Inter-American Conferences

Conference on the Maintenance of Peace: Buenos Aires, 1936

An Additional Protocol on Nonintervention was approved which stressed various of the principles supported in Montevideo three years before, as well as a Declaration of Principles of Inter-American Solidarity and Cooperation. However, the most important action of the meeting was probably the agreement to create a consultative mechanism which would operate in case of a threat to American security through war or other acts of aggression.

Conference on Problems of War and Peace: Mexico, 1945

Two main political documents were approved at this conference: The Act of Chapultepec and the Declaration of Mexico. These ratified various legal and political principles formulated at previous meetings. The proposals of Dumbarton Oaks on the System of the Organization of Nations, which was to be established the following year in San Francisco, were accepted with certain Latin-American reservations. The Economic Charter of the Americas was approved. Its purpose was to facilitate economic development and the normalization of trade in the postwar period. This document, in particular, gave rise to a clash between the interests of the great United States monopolies and the desire of broad sectors of Latin-American opinion for rapid development.

Conference for the Maintenance of Continental Peace and Security: Quintandinha (Rio de Janeiro), 1947

The Inter-American Treaty of Reciprocal Assistance was signed, involving a profound transformation of the Pan-American organization which was made to conform to the principles of the Charter of the United Nations. By way of symbolic compensation for the political and military obligations assumed, the Latin-American governments brought pressure to bear to elicit sympathy from the United States for their economic problems, in order to increase financing through loans and direct investments.

Special Conference of the Inter-American Economic and Social Council at the Ministerial Level: Punta del Este, Uruguay, 1961
At this meeting, the so-called Declaration of the Peoples of America and the program known as the Alliance for Progress were adopted. These postulated the advisability of (1) carrying out certain institutional reforms (land, tax, educational, administrative, etc.); (2) obtaining greater external financing and more favorable commercial treatment from the industrial countries; and (3) planning and accelerating Latin-American economic integration.

First Extraordinary Conference: Washington, 1964
The essential purpose of this conference was to discuss the requirements for admission of new members to the OAS. Articles 2 and 108 of the Bogotá Charter were ratified and the importance reiterated of fulfilling the collective hemisphere security obligations (Articles 24 and 25 of the Charter) and, particularly, of signing and ratifying the Inter-American Reciprocal Assistance Treaty of 1947.

Second Extraordinary Conference: Rio de Janeiro, 1965
The intervention of the United States in Santo Domingo had grave consequences. Even the customarily docile Latin-American governments showed their concern and censured the behavior of the United States in one form or another. The United States immediately sought the proper occasion for redressing matters and found it at this conference. The aggression against the Dominican Republic was not even mentioned there, in return for which there was no insistence upon the establishment of the Inter-American Peace Force, and the criticisms of the OAS were answered by an agreement to revise the Bogotá Charter and to place greater stress upon certain forms of economic cooperation.

Third Extraordinary Conference: Buenos Aires, 1967
Its purpose was to revise the Charter of the Organization of American States. The main amendments consisted of revising and broadening the section of Economic Regulations, giving the permanent Council greater powers, substituting a General Assembly

like that of the United Nations for the traditional irregular inter-American conferences, and establishing, together with the Economic and Social Council, an agency of equal scope for Education, Science and Culture. The advisability of promoting economic programming and integration was reiterated; and emphasis was given to the importance of collective or supranational action within the Pan-American framework. In other words, the Buenos Aires conference successfully utilized one of its severest crises to bolster the OAS.

Consultative Meetings

First Meeting: Panama, 1939
A Joint Declaration of Continental Solidarity was signed which in large part ratified the Lima Declaration. The possible consequences to America from an incipient World War II were discussed, but it was, nevertheless, reiterated that the governments would act "... independently in their individual capacity with full recognition of their legal equality as sovereign states."

Second Meeting: Havana, 1940
It was recommended that differences and disputes among the countries of America be settled. In the Havana Act, the possibility was foreseen of establishing a temporary system of protection for the American colonies and possessions of European countries through the adoption of a Resolution (XV) on Reciprocal Assistance and Cooperation, which provided that in case of acts or danger of aggression "on the part of a non-American state" against an American state "... the signatory states of the . . . Declaration will consult with each other in order to decide upon the proper measures to be taken."

A resolution on economic and financial cooperation was approved.

Third Meeting: Rio de Janeiro, 1942
The creation of the Inter-American Defense Board was approved; it was to have the function of studying and recommending to American governments the necessary measures for the defense of the continent. Also approved was the establishment of the Emergency Advisory Committee for Political Defense for the purpose of combating the subversive activities of the Nazis. The

Inter-American Juridical Committee was reorganized and the functions of the Inter-American Financial and Economic Advisory Committee were broadened.

Fourth Meeting: Washington, 1951

The Inter-American Defense Board was reinforced by imposing greater subordination of Latin America to the war policy of the United States, then engaged in its aggression upon Korea. Various resolutions were adopted on political, economic, and military cooperation because of the state of emergency decreed in Washington as a result of the supposed aggression of international Communism. The Washington Declaration reaffirmed the solidarity of the Latin-American governments with the Cold War policy openly adopted by the United States in 1946.

Conflicts of jurisdiction between the OAS and the UN were discussed and an emergency economic cooperation program was agreed upon in which an attempt was made, obviously to the advantage of the United States, to combine its immediate procurement of the maximum supply of raw materials and commodities with the traditional aspiration to long-term economic development of the other countries of the hemisphere.

Fifth Meeting: Santiago, Chile, 1959

Worried by the crushing victory of the Cuban Revolution and by the radical and nationalist character of the measures adopted by the Cuban government, the other governments of the continent vigorously defended "representative democracy" in the Santiago Declaration, and anti-Communist declarations mounted. The Inter-American Peace Committee was charged with keeping a check on the Caribbean situation and issuing a warning, without delay, in case it worsened. (During that time, the Cuban government denounced a joint invasion attempt by the overthrown dictator, Batista, and the perennial President of the Dominican Republic, General Trujillo.)

Sixth Meeting: San José, Costa Rica, 1960

The main purpose of this meeting was to investigate Venezuelan charges against the Trujillo government of the Dominican Republic. On the basis of a report from the Inter-American Peace Committee, the Dominican government was condemned by a wide majority for acts of intervention and aggression against Venezuela, and sanctions were imposed on it: diplomatic relations were severed and all shipments of arms and implements of war were immediately suspended. The United States was at first opposed to applying sanctions but finally adopted the position of the other countries represented.

Seventh Meeting: San José, Costa Rica, 1960

The United States denounced the installation of a Communist government as the equivalent of loss of independence by a country and as a grave danger to hemispheric security. Within the framework of these concepts, the Declaration of San José condemned the intervention of an extra-continental power in American affairs, and condemned as acts of aggression against the security of America, the attempts of the Sino-Soviet powers to take advantage of the position of an American country favorable to them. The Declaration also reaffirmed the mandatory nature of the principles adopted in Santiago (1959) with regard to representative democracy.

Actually, the meeting was nothing more than another episode in the anti-Communist crusade and a new attempt—the most determined up to that time—to prevent Cuba from carrying out a true social revolution. For that reason, the Cuban government accused the consultative organ of the OAS of intervening with no right whatsoever in the affairs of other countries and of violating the right of self-determination of nations.

Eighth Meeting: Punta del Este, Uruguay, 1962

The struggle against the Cuban Revolution promoted by the United States came to a head at the Eighth Meeting of Foreign Ministers. In 1960, Cuba was branded a threat to continental security. In 1961, when the revolutionary process crystallized in an unprecedented social transformation, United States imperialism launched its unsuccessful Bay of Pigs invasion. And, several months later, at the Eighth Consultative Meeting, the OAS declared Cuba incompatible with Pan-Americanism and the principles of "representative democracy." Never in the long history of Latin-American "gorillarchies" had a government been excluded from the OAS system for its undemocratic character. Yet when the small country of Cuba decided to reconstitute its sovereignty and, in the exercise thereof, to take forceful measures which affected the United States monopolies and the insignificant minority of wealthy Cubans, its action provoked greater hostility than the Mexican and Guatemalan revolutions in their time.

Ninth Meeting: Washington, 1964

On the basis of an alleged aggression upon Venezuela by Cuba, it was agreed to sanction Cuba under the Rio de Janeiro Treaty. Actually this treaty was shamelessly invoked not in defense against an "armed attack" or other aggression but to prevent a country from instituting the type of government and even the social system of its choice. Until 1964, all American nations could theoretically determine their own fate and organize their public life as they saw fit. After the Ninth Meeting of Foreign Ministers, however, it was made clear that what had traditionally been a right was now a crime, a serious threat to hemispheric solidarity. So-called representative democracy, with its abject attitude toward imperialism, foreign investors, and local military strong men, had inevitably become the accepted form of government, and the only one in harmony with the strict rules of Pan-Americanism.

Tenth Meeting: Washington, 1965
Although this meeting was held during the critical days of the aggression against the Dominican Republic by the United States, nobody protested against it in time or with any firmness. The foreign ministers limited themselves to setting up a commission of representatives from five countries whose function was to report on the Dominican situation and help re-establish "peace and normalcy." It was likewise agreed to "request the member governments so desiring and in a position to do so, that they provide the OAS . . . with land, sea, air, or police forces to be used to integrate an inter-American force which would operate under the authority of this Tenth Consultative Meeting."

Eleventh Meeting: Buenos Aires, 1967
The main task of this meeting was the organization of the Meeting of Presidents of American Countries held in Punta del Este in April, 1967, and the selection of topics and preparation of the principal texts to be taken up there. The Meeting of Presidents served in large measure to demonstrate the unity of the governments with relation to the principles of Pan-Americanism and to fortify the OAS.

Twelfth Meeting: Washington, 1967
A new accusation against Cuba by Venezuela gave rise to this meeting at which violent anti-Communism was again manifested. Resolution 3, one of the principal resolutions of the meeting, vigorously condemned "the present government of Cuba for its repeated acts of aggression and intervention against Venezuela and for its policy of intervention in the internal affairs of Bolivia and other American states . . ." The Tricontinental Conference and

OLAS were denounced as instruments of Communism which threatened the security of America, and the governments having commercial and diplomatic relations with Cuba were asked to take part in what is a *de facto* boycott against it.

Appendix II

Resolutions of the First Latin-American Solidarity Conference

The First Conference of the Latin-American Solidarity Organization (OLAS), held in Havana between July 31 and August 10, 1967, was attended by 164 delegates from 28 countries, approximately 100 observers, and 281 newspapermen from 38 countries.

Fundamental problems of Latin America were taken up at the conference, which adopted three general resolutions, a number of agreements on specific points, and a General Declaration which may be said to sum up and underscore the main questions raised in the debates. The resolutions and the General Declaration are contained in a closely printed text of 63 pages, impossible to reproduce here.

However, in view of the fact that these documents represent a faithful image of the aspirations for independence of the peoples of Latin America and their rejection of Pan-Americanism and imperialism, I have prepared a brief summary, selecting the most important ones and using as much of the original texts as possible.

General Resolution on the Revolutionary Struggle in Latin America
• Present historical conditions are favorable to the revolutionary forces and unfavorable to those of imperialism. . . . The revolutionary movements of the last decades show that revolution is possible when the people follow the correct course and have the support of a militant vanguard.
• The Cuban Revolution destroyed the myths of geographical determinism and of the invincibility of imperialism. Its victory constitutes an example, a source of encouragement, and a factor in advancing revolutionary struggle in Latin America.
• Imperialism is striving by every means possible to prevent another Cuba from emerging: espionage networks, police organizations, armed aggression, the subservience of the oligarchies, attempts to create a permanent inter-American force. . . . Its underlying purpose is to stop the advance of revolutionary struggle

179

throughout the world. . . . In spite of its military power, it is, nevertheless, beginning to reveal its inability to crush the struggle of the people, as the Vietnam War so eloquently demonstrates.

• The revolutionary potential of the peoples of the continent against imperialism is gathering strength: a strong and militant proletariat in the big cities, a vast mass of poor and brutally exploited peasants . . . a new and youthful intellectual element . . . a student group with a splendid tradition of struggle . . . and intermediate strata more closely allied to the people than to oligarchy and imperialism. . . . The Latin-American bourgeoisie is part of the oligarchy . . . its action does not go beyond the limits set for it by imperialism and only in isolated instances can certain sectors play a positive role if they join the forces of liberation.

• As the revolutionary process sharpens, the oligarchy in turn consolidates around imperialism and lends itself to its continental strategy. . . . As a consequence, the people have no other alternative than to fight reactionary violence with revolutionary violence.

• The primary objective of the revolution on the continent is the seizure of power through the destruction of the bureaucratic and military apparatus of the state and its replacement by the power of the people for the purpose of changing the existing socio-economic system. . . . The common political strategy should be to sharpen the class struggle and resort to armed struggle as the basic path of liberation.

• The vanguard status of the people is the result of the determination to struggle, to lead, and to carry revolutionary action forward to its ultimate consequences. . . . The vanguards will be those who point out and develop the true pathways of the revolution. . . . Experience shows the incalculable importance of effective, courageous, determined, steadfast, and intelligent leadership.

• Because of its broad geographic extension, its topographical characteristics, and the exploitation suffered by the peasant population, the countryside is the fundamental theater of struggle and the milieu in which it is possible to conduct the most important class combats. . . . This is true, as well, because modern armies and the repression of popular movements are more effective in the cities. Of course, the role of the urban population and, particularly, of the working class in the revolutionary struggle should not be underestimated.

Resolution on the Mechanisms of Economic Penetration

• Imperialistic and colonial exploitation is the cause of the backwardness, stagnation, and deformation of the economy of Latin America. For the eradication of underdevelopment and the liberation of millions of human beings from hunger, disease, ignorance, and lack of culture, it is essential that this exploitation be brought to an end.

• Military dictatorships are not the result of spontaneous generation but the product of underdevelopment, foreign dependence, and the structure of neo-colonial exploitation.

• True Latin-American integration is possible only through new and revolutionary international division of labor.

• The Latin-American bourgeoisie cannot lead the struggle for emancipation. . . . It is subservient to imperialism. Only the united and organized popular masses are capable of breaking up the outgrown structures that prevent development.

Resolution on the Politico-Military Intervention of the United States on the Continent

• In order to repress popular struggles in Latin America, United States imperialism has established an overall strategy of unifying military and police forces which utilize, among other means, the establishment of sea and air bases in violation of national sovereignty, and its Department of Colonies, the OAS.

• The United States is able to use the aid of other imperialist powers in order to strengthen its positions and now has under way the training of Latin-American military cadres, advised by Yankee officers. The so-called Inter-American Peace Force may turn out to be the culmination of the OAS.

• The continental scope of the politico-military framework of the United States calls for the opposition of a common revolutionary strategy on the part of the Latin-American people. . . .

Cultural and Ideological Penetration of United States Imperialism in Latin America

• Imperialism seeks to broaden its influence in the fields of education, scientific research, the arts, and the labor, peasant, and student movements, through dominating the mass media (press, radio, comics, television, international information agencies, etc.). It systematically distorts the truth through all these means, by the introduction of values contrary to the best interests of our peoples, and tastes and styles which deform national culture.

• In the fields of education and scientific research, imperialism seeks to subordinate the universities and institutes to its policy, using for the purpose sociological research projects such as

Camelot and "Simpático" and the activities of the Peace Corps.
. . . It penetrates student and worker organizations through fellow-
ships, subsidies, and exchange trips, and seeks to corrupt the best
revolutionary traditions of the Latin-American peoples.

• Important as they are, the courageous struggles of teachers,
students, and intellectuals are insufficient for eradicating that
penetration. *It is the duty of every revolutionary to make revolution.* The revolution is made by the people, the great exploited
masses. Intellectual workers are part of the people. . . . Their
higher intellectual level is a privilege, but, more than anything
else, a responsibility. . . .

In addition to participating through their works, intellectuals
must join the revolutionary struggle and incorporate their efforts
into new mechanisms on a Latin-American scale.

Resolution on the OAS

• The favorite instrument of United States imperialism for
carrying out its interventionist policy in Latin America is the so-
called Organization of American States.

• The OAS has never intervened in cases of aggression by imperialism and when it has done so, it has been only for the purpose
of legitimatizing them through crude, pseudo-legal devices. This
was made evident by the October "crisis," the blockade of Cuba,
and the United States military intervention in the Dominican
Republic.

• The Latin-American peoples have the right and the duty to
combat the decisions of the OAS.

General Resolution on Action against the Politico-Military Inter-vention and the Economic and Ideological Penetration of Im-perialism in Latin America

• The formulation of a common political strategy of struggle for
our peoples is essential, a strategy based on the fact that United
States imperialism is the fundamental enemy. . . . Division has
always been the best ally of colonialism and imperialism. . . . The
struggle for national liberation in each country of Latin America
should be considered part of the overall struggle of the continent.

• Our revolutionary process embraces all forms of struggle, but
the highest and most fundamental form in Latin America is that
of armed struggle. . . . The only possible path is that of developing
and deepening the revolutionary struggle to the point of a war of
liberation against imperialism and the ruling classes. . . .

General Resolution on the Solidarity of the Latin-American Peoples
• The advancement of the revolutionary struggle within each country is the fundamental expression of solidarity. That solidarity should reach its culmination in the basic form of taking power: armed struggle.
• Solidarity is part of the common struggle of the people in retaliation for the repressive continental strategy of imperialism, and it calls for the forward impetus of armed struggle . . . through the presence of revolutionary fighters of any country where the struggle may be going on. Solidarity is also manifested through material aid and supporting political activity.
• The Latin-American revolution is closely tied to the freedom movements of the peoples of Asia, Africa, of the labor movement of the capitalist countries, of the Negro people of the United States, and of all men who fight for the liberation of the people.
• The Latin-American revolutionary movement calls for solidarity and maximum aid on the part of the countries which have been freed from capitalist exploitation.
• The best form that solidarity with Cuba can take is that of giving effective aid to the armed revolutionary movement of our respective countries.

Other Resolutions
In addition to the above, the First Conference of OLAS adopted specific resolutions on various topics intended mainly to express Latin-American solidarity with other peoples. It was agreed to support the struggle of the Negro people in the United States, of the African peoples for full independence, of the Arab peoples, of the Asiatic peoples, of the Colombian, Guatemalan, Venezuelan, and Bolivian guerrillas, and the heroic defense of the people of Vietnam against imperialism. A greeting was sent to the Soviet Union on the 50th anniversary of the October Revolution, another to Comandante Che Guevara, and a General Declaration was approved, the salient points of which are listed below.

General Declaration
1. It is the right and the duty of the people of Latin America to make revolution. The Latin-American revolution has roots going deep into the past and today's struggles have their inspiration in that glorious history. The Latin-American revolution is a struggle for national independence, emancipation from the oligarchies, and for the socialist road to full economic and social development. The

principles of Marxism-Leninism are the guide for the Latin-American revolution.

2. The revolutionary armed struggle is the fundamental line of the revolution. Other forms should serve to advance the fundamental line. The immediate and principal task of the majority of the countries of the continent is to organize, initiate, and develop the armed struggle. The responsibility of advancing the revolution belongs to the people of each country and their vanguards. The guerrillas—as liberation armies in embryo—are the most effective means of advancing the revolutionary struggle in most countries. The direction of the revolution calls for a unified political and military command.

3. The most effective solidarity is the advancement of the revolutionary struggle in each country. Solidarity with Cuba and with armed movements is a duty of the anti-imperialist organizations that they cannot fail to assume.

The Cuban Revolution is the vanguard of the Latin-American anti-imperialist movement.

4. The Second Havana Declaration sets forth the program for the Latin-American Revolution.

Colonial peoples, strictly speaking, who are ruled by European powers or by the United States must fight for their independence and keep themselves closely linked to the general struggle of the continent.

The peoples of Latin America bear no hostility toward other peoples and fraternally exhort the people of the United States, itself, to fight against imperialist monopolies.

The peoples of Latin America express their solidarity with the peoples of Asia and Africa, with the workers of the capitalist countries, with the socialist countries, and with the Negro people of the United States. The heroic struggle of the Vietnamese people is an aid and an example for the peoples of Latin America.

Selected Bibliography

Abreu Gómez, Ermilo, "Farsa concluida," *Política*, Mexico, February 15, 1962.

Aguilar, Alonso, *La política económica de la revolución cubana*, Mexico, 1959.

———, *Latin America and the Alliance for Progress*, New York, 1963.

Alberdi, Juan Bautista, "Conveniencia y objetos de un congreso general americano," *Hispanoamérica en lucha por su independencia*, Jesús Silva Herzog, ed., Mexico, 1962.

Arévalo, Juan José, *Guatemala, la democracia, y el imperio*, Mexico, 1954.

Barcia Trelles, Camilo, *Doctrina de Monroe y cooperación internacional*, Madrid, 1931.

———, *La política exterior norteamericana de la postguerra*, Valladolid, 1924.

Bassols, Narciso, "¿Alianza automática? Desgraciadamente, sí," *El Universal*, October 6, 1947.

———, *Obras*, Mexico, 1964.

Bolívar, Simón, *Obras Completas*, vol. II.

Bowers, Claude G., *Beveridge and the Progressive Era*, New York, 1932.

Cabrera, Luis (Blas Urrea), *Una opinión mexicana sobre el conflicto mundial*, Mexico, 1951.

Campos Ortiz, Pablo, "Bases constitucionales de la OEA," *México en la IX conferencia internacional americana*, Mexico, 1948.

Cardoza y Aragón, Luis, "La conferencia de cancilleres: Su significación para América Latina," *Cuadernos Americanos*, Mexico, May–June, 1951.

———, *La revolución guatemalteca*, Montevideo, 1956.

Carrillo Flores, Antonio, "El problema de las inversiones extranjeras," *México en la IX conferencia internacional americana*, Mexico, 1948.

Castro, Fidel, "La historia me absolverá," *La revolución cubana*, Havana, n.d.

185

Cuevas Cancino, Francisco, *Bolívar: El ideal panamericano del libertador*, Mexico, 1951.

El financiamiento externo de América Latina, United Nations Economic Commission for Latin America (ECLA), New York, 1964.

Fabela, Isidro, *Cartas al presidente Cárdenas*, Mexico, 1947.

——, *Intervención*, Mexico, 1959.

——, *La conferencia de Caracas y la actitud anticomunista de México*, Mexico, 1954.

——, *Los Estados Unidos y la 'América Latina (1921–1929)*, Mexico, 1955.

Frondizi, Arturo, *Industria argentina y desarrollo nacional*, Buenos Aires, 1957.

Gerassi, John, *The Great Fear*, New York, 1963.

Hernández Solís, Luis, *El panamericanismo. Una moderna interpretación*, Mexico, 1944.

Huberman, Leo, *We, the People*, New York, 1947 (reprinted New York, 1964).

"Imperialismo y buena vecindad" (mesa rodante), *Cuadernos Americanos*, Mexico, September-October, 1947.

Ingenieros, José, "Por la unión latinamericana," *Hispanoamérica en lucha por su independencia*, Jesús Silva Herzog, ed., Mexico, 1962.

Jenks, Leland W., *Our Cuban Colony*, New York, 1928.

Kepner, C. D., Jr., and Soothill, J. H., *El imperio del banano*, Buenos Aires, 1957.

"La reunión de cancilleres," *Cuadernos Americanos*, Mexico, May-June, 1951.

Le Riverend, Julio, *Historia económica de Cuba*, Havana, 1963.

Lewis, Gordon K., *Puerto Rico: Freedom and Power in the Caribbean*, New York, 1963.

Lieuwen, Edwin, *Arms and Politics in Latin America*, New York, 1960.

Link, Arthur S., *La política de Estados Unidos en América Latina (1913–1916)*, Mexico, 1960.

Lippmann, Walter, *U.S. Foreign Policy: Shield of the Republic*, Boston, 1943.

Loyo, Gilberto, "El convenio económico de Bogotá," *México en la IX conferencia internacional americana*, Mexico, 1948.

Machado, Eduardo, *Las primeras agresiones del imperialismo contra Venezuela*, Mexico, 1957.

Marion, George, *Bases and Empire*, New York, 1948.

Martí, José, *El universo en Martí*, Ministerio de relaciones exteriores de Cuba, n.d.

Martínez, Ricardo A., *El panamericanismo, doctrina y práctica imperialista*, Buenos Aires, 1957.

Martínez de la Vega, Francisco, "¿Amigo de todos? Amigo de nadie," *Siempre*, Mexico, December, 1965.

Mecham, Lloyd, *The United States and Inter-American Security, 1889–1960*, Texas, 1961.

Montenegro, Carlos, *Las inversiones extranjeras en América Latina*, Buenos Aires, 1962.

Nearing, Scott and Freeman, Joseph, *Dollar Diplomacy*, New York, 1925 (reprinted New York, 1966).

Olden, Herman, *U.S. Over Latin America*, New York, 1955.

Pendle, George, *A History of Latin America*, London, 1963.

Perlo, Victor, *American Imperialism*, New York, 1951.

"Primera conferencia de solidaridad de los pueblos de Asia, Africa y América Latina," *Cuba Socialista*, Havana, February, 1966.

Readings in American Foreign Policy, Robert A. Goldwin, Ralph Lerner, Gerald Stourah, eds., New York, 1959.

Reyes Heroles, Jesús, *La carta de la Habana*, Mexico, 1948.

Roa, Raúl, *Retorno a la Alborada*, vol. II, Havana, 1964.

Roosevelt, Franklin D., *Nothing to Fear. The Selected Addresses of F. D. Roosevelt, 1932–1945*, New York, 1946.

———, *The Public Papers and Addresses of FDR*, Vol. 8, New York, 1941.

Sáenz Peña, Roque, "La Doctrina Monroe y su evolución," *Hispanoamérica en lucha por su independencia*, Jesús Silva Herzog, ed., Mexico, 1962.

Scott, James Brown, *The International Conferences of American States, 1889–1928*, New York, 1931.

Silva Herzog, Jesús, "Mi cuarto a espadas," *Cuadernos Americanos*, Mexico, May-June, 1951.

Smith, Robert A., *Your Foreign Policy*, New York, 1941.

Toriello, Guillermo, *La Batalla de Guatemala*, Mexico, 1955.

Torras, Pelegrín, "La segunda conferencia interamericana extraordinaria," *Cuba Socialista*, January, 1966.

Turner, David M., *Estructura económica de Panamá*, Mexico, 1958.

Waiss, Oscar, *Nacionalismo y socialismo en América Latina*, Buenos Aires, 1961.

Wise, David and Ross, Thomas B., *The Invisible Government*, New York, 1964.

Index

DATE DUE